A Horseman's Handbook

Rachael Kydd

Long Distance Riding Explained

Arco Publishing Company, Inc.
New York

Horseman's Handbooks

TRAINING EXPLAINED
JUMPING EXPLAINED
STABLE MANAGEMENT EXPLAINED
DRESSAGE EXPLAINED
EVENTING EXPLAINED
TACK EXPLAINED
MY PONY
SHOWDRIVING EXPLAINED
SHOWING AND RINGCRAFT EXPLAINED
HORSE AILMENTS EXPLAINED
HORSE AND PONY BREEDING EXPLAINED

We are grateful to the following for kindly providing photographs for this book —
Colour photographs: Charles Barieau (pages 17, 18 and 27); Keith Stevens (pages 29
and 40); Dianne Gillies (page 30); Val Males (pages 39, 57 and 58 above); Dr Valerie
Noli-Marais (pages 58 below, 67 and 68); Kit Houghton (pages 69, 70 above, 79 and
80 above); Dr Robert Marshall (page 70 below); Mary Bancroft (page 80 below); and
Martin Rice-Edwards (page 28). *Black and white photographs*: Charles Barieau (pages
6 above, 34 and 44); Levi Strauss and Co (pages 15, 82, 84 and 86); Dr Robert Marshall (page 10); Ern McQuillan (page 21); Dianne Gillies (page 88); Val Males (pages
32, 54, 60, 73 below and 87); and Martin Rice-Edwards (frontispiece and page 73 above).
Jacket photograph: Dr Robert Marshall. The jacket photograph shows the Golden
Horseshoe Ride, on Exmoor, south-west England.

First published in Great Britain in 1979
by Ward Lock Limited, a Pentos Company.

Published 1979 by Arco Publishing
Company, Inc. 219 Park Avenue South,
New York, N.Y. 10003

**Library of Congress Cataloging in
Publication Data**
Kydd, Rachael.
    Long distance riding explained.
    (A Horseman's handbook)
    1. Endurance riding (Horsemanship). 2. Trial riding
—Competitions. I. Title. II. Series.
SF296.E5K93   798'.23   78-8998
ISBN 0-668-04579-5
ISBN 0-668-04583-3 pbk.

Printed in Great Britain by
T. & A. Constable Ltd, Edinburgh

Previous page The general scene at a halt on an endurance ride in the USA.

Contents

Acknowledgements

I wish here to thank Minette Rice-Edwards, without whose help I would have found it impossible to write this book and to whom it is gratefully dedicated. Mrs. Rice-Edwards is an English horsewoman who spent six years in the United States where she learnt much about long distance riding and greatly enjoyed the friendly companionship of her competitors. Her aim was to ride in the Tevis and finish with her horse in superlative condition. This she did in 1973, taking 12 hours 51 minutes — the fourth fastest time — so that her mare Bright Hope won the Haggin Cup. Much of the advice which follows, on training and riding the ride, is based on Minette Rice-Edwards' experience. I am grateful to her both for the hours she spent talking to me before I even started to write and for the time she gave to reading and commenting on two successive drafts. My debt is increased by the fact that she herself is planning a book on training the long distance horse; a less generous person would not have allowed another author to use her experience so freely.

I am equally grateful to Ron and Val Males of Australia. They took many photographs at my request, supplied much essential information, read the typescript, made many helpful suggestions and several corrections. Ron has ridden in six Quilties and Val in three; together they breed endurance horses on their Arab stud.

I have also to thank Chuck and Marty Stephens who took me to visit the Quilty course, for which Chuck is responsible; Brian Eagles M.R.C.V.S. who gave up a whole afternoon to discuss the veterinary problems, but who is not responsible for any of the errors this book may contain; Pamela du Boulay for the legend in Figure 2; Pitman Publishing who allowed the use of Figures 1 and 2; James Fleming who read the first draft (much to its benefit); and Jane Turner, herself a long distance rider, who performed the miracle of transmuting my first draft into an intelligible typescript.

Introduction

What is Long Distance Riding?

The subject discussed in this book does not include journeys on horseback planned by the rider himself, nor riding holidays planned for him by commercial organizations and sometimes called trekking, but only the kind of long distance riding which can be described as sport. This we shall consider as it is practised in the United States, Australia, Britain and South Africa.

How long is long distance? The shortest distance considered 'long' by a long distance riding society appears to be 15 miles (24 km). Many people may find it difficult to regard this as long unless it is ridden very fast. It is no further than they might go on an ordinary morning's hack and much less far than during a day's hunting. Even 40 or 50 miles (64-80 km) in a day was not a long ride for our ancestors, nor is it now for those who, like New Zealanders and Australians, still use horses to work with sheep and cattle. The fact is that 'long distance' is a relative term — relative not only to the speed at which the ground is covered but to the distance usually travelled by a particular rider and a particular horse. Fifteen miles, or even 20 or 25 (24, 32 or 40 km), do not require a special horse or special training, but they are still a long way for an animal straight off grass carrying an unfit rider on a hot summer's day.

Many more people are able to take part in long distance riding than in the more highly specialized forms of equestrian sport. The long hours spent together in unfamiliar places create a special sort of understanding between horse and rider and sharing in a contest which is mainly against natural forces creates comradeship amongst the riders.

The buckle awarded to all who 'complete' the Tevis. (USA)
The buckle awarded to all who 'complete' the Quilty. (Australia)

1 The different kinds of long distance ride

Anyone interested in long distance riding needs to know how one kind of ride differs from another and what rules apply to each. Here a difficulty arises. Since there is no world organization to co-ordinate the sport, which even in Britain is run by several separate societies, there is no universal terminology.

In Britain the terms 'long distance riding' and 'endurance riding' are often used interchangeably. Thus the Endurance Horse and Pony Society is a long distance organization planning rides of several different types. But in the United States and Australia the term 'endurance' is applied only to rides of one particular type. Australia has no general term equivalent to the British 'long distance riding'. In the United States the general term is 'trail riding'; trail rides being divided into 'endurance trail rides', 'competitive trail rides' and 'pleasure trail rides'. The term 'race' also presents difficulties. For many years most English speaking countries have been loath to use 'race' in the title or official description of a long distance ride. This is because many horses died in the European long distance races at the turn of the century. None the less, all rides where the winner is the horse with the fastest time are often referred to unofficially as races in the United States. In Britain this term tends to be reserved for rides where the winner does not need to finish 'fit to continue', but only 'not ill-used'.

The classification which follows may not seem acceptable to everybody. But it is not possible to explain long distance riding until some classification has been made.

Long Distance Rides are basically of three types:

A Rides with a winner who completes the course in the shortest time.

B Rides which are competitive, but where speed is not the only criterion of success.

C Organized rides which have no competitive aim.

Type A is divided into:

Endurance Rides. In these, horses not fit to continue at the finish are disqualified.

Long Distance Races. In these, veterinary inspection at the finish is limited to establishing that the horses have not been ill-used.

Ride and Tie Races. In these, each competing partnership is made up of one horse and two humans, the latter running and riding alternately.

Type B is divided into:

Trials. In these, competitors are placed in an order of merit which is judged partly on the speed at which they have completed the course and partly under a number of other headings.

Tests. In these, competitors are not placed in an order of merit. Their performance is judged against a standard or set of standards, and they are graded accordingly.

Type A

Endurance Rides

These are basically races in which the horses are protected by being required to conform to standards of fitness and well-being throughout. What these standards are and how they are applied is the main subject of Chapter 6, but here it is necessary to mention certain salient points. All horses must pass a veterinary inspection before the start; they must also pass other such inspections at compulsory resting halts (see Glossary), and sometimes also at spot-checks along the route, and a final inspection at the finish. Here they must be in a condition which is variously, and nearly always ambiguously, described in the ride rules. Most of these say that the horse must be 'in fit condition to continue', without specifying for how far; some merely state that he should be 'in sufficient condition', not specifying for what.

All endurance rides have some additional rules. How many depends on whether or not the organizers believe that competitors should be left as free as possible. These rules concern the eligibility of horse and rider; what minimum weight, if any, the horse should be required to carry; what saddlery and clothing must or must not be worn; what drugs, medicaments and other artificial aids may or may not be used, and the manner in which horses and riders should behave.

Eligibility of horse and rider   Most rules state that the horse must have reached a minimum age, usually 5, by the time of the ride, a few that he must not be over a maximum age, some that he must be over a minimum height. Some ban pregnant mares. Some require that the rider shall have reached a certain age; others allow younger riders to compete provided they are accompanied throughout by an accepted, responsible adult. Some of the longer rides specify that horses, or riders, or both, should have successfully completed a shorter ride, chosen from an approved list, in the recent past.

Weights   Some rides have no weight requirements. Some fix a minimum which all horses must carry, some a minimum which must be carried by winning and placed horses but not by those to be rewarded simply for completing the course. Some rides split their entrants into two or more weight divisions and make separate awards in each.

Saddlery and clothes   Some rides allow a horse to compete unsaddled, or unshod, or both, others do not. Many prohibit spurs and some whips. Some demand that the rider should wear a hard hat, or footwear with heels, or both. More information on these points will be found in Chapter 4.

Drugs, medicaments and artificial aids   The use of drugs as

9

The start of the 1976 Arab Horse Society Marathon Race. (Britain)

stimulants and tranquillizers is usually prohibited; pain killers are sometimes allowed, liniments nearly always. Supportive bandages are usually permitted, but some rides do not allow overreach or brushing boots.

Behaviour   Some rules give the organizers power to eliminate horses whose behaviour endangers other horses or people, or riders who damage property, or who trespass on to land where riding is not permitted.

Awards   Although all endurance rides present their major trophy to the horse which finishes in the shortest time — the winner — most offer an important second award judged on finishing condition. The horses eligible for this must also make good time, either finishing among the first 5 or the first 10 or within a fixed percentage of the time taken by the winner. Completing the ride is nearly always itself a considerable achievement and is the sole aim of most competitors. In the United States and Australia the traditional reward for this is a Buckle (see photo page 6). The time allowed is not unlimited, but is a great deal longer than that of the fastest horse.

Length of ride.   One day rides vary in length from 50 miles to about 110 (80-176 km). Two day rides are usually divided 50-50 (80-80) in the United States; at least one in Australia is divided 100-20 (160-32). Three day rides are not common, but one such in South Africa is divided 50-50-31 (80-80-50). Longer rides, usually spread over five or six days were the rule before World War II. Though these no longer form part of any annual programme, from time to time one is organized to mark a special occasion. Thus in 1975 the 600 miles (960 km) from Sydney to Melbourne were ridden in fourteen days (two being compulsory rests) for the première of the film *Bite the Bullet.*

All rides are divided up by compulsory halts. These are usually spaced 25 to 30 miles (40-48 km) apart. Obligatory time at halts is normally either half an hour or one hour.

The time which a competitor takes to go from start to finish is called his *total elapsed time;* this, minus the time he is obliged to spend at halts, is called his *riding time.* Twenty four hours total elapsed time is usually, but not always, allowed for the completion of 100 miles (160 km).

Speeds vary with the course, climate and current weather conditions. Flat country, springy turf and a cool, crisp day provide conditions for the fastest speeds; hilly country, yielding going (soft sand or mud), and a hot, humid day reduce speeds to the slowest. Speeds made in similar conditions in different countries may vary greatly because riders in some are more experienced than riders in others. In the United States it is not unusual for a 100 mile (160 km) one day ride to be ridden at an average speed of 12 mph (19 kph) and a 50 mile (80 km) ride at 15 mph (24kph) — time at halts deducted. These speeds cannot be achieved in Britain before riders become more experienced in both choosing and training their horses.

Examples of leading rides — United States   Here the principle ride is the Western States Trail Ride for the Tevis Cup —

The Tevis. This has been run annually since 1955. The route covers 100 miles (160 km), climbs a total of 9050 ft (2578 m) and falls a total of 15205 ft (4634 m). The altitude varies between 1000 and 7430 ft (305 and 2264 m). In places climatic conditions greatly add to the difficulty of the route; in the canyons, familiarly known as 'the bake ovens', the temperature is 100°F (35°C) or over and the relative humidity very high. This ride is divided by four halts, one of half an hour and three of an hour. The winner, who must finish 'in condition to go on' and carry 165 lbs (74·8 kg), is awarded the Tevis Cup. The horse 'in most superior condition to go on' also carrying 165 lbs and finishing among the fastest ten is awarded the Haggin Cup. All competitors who complete the ride within $21\frac{1}{2}$ hours riding time 'in condition to go on' are awarded Tevis Buckles —irrespective of what weight they are carrying. In 1978 198 competitors started and 132 'completed the ride'. For a summary of the results 1955-1978 see Appendix 1. In 1977 144 endurance rides were sanctioned by the American Endurance Ride Conference. Not all endurance organizations are affiliated to this body.

Australia   Here the principle ride is the Tom Quilty Endurance 100 mile (160 km) Ride — The Quilty. This has been run annually since 1966. The route was partially changed in 1978 and now measures not 100 but 108 miles (173 km). The old route climbed 8000 ft (2438 m) and fell 10,000 (3048 m). The heights climbed and descended in 1978 were considerably in excess of this but have not yet been measured since further changes in the route will be made. Riders have to qualify. All horses must carry 160 lbs (72·5 kg). 'Whips and spurs are not allowed at all'. Riders may choose 'clothing or equipment to suit themselves'. The winner, who must pass the vet. at the end of the ride, is awarded the Tom Quilty Gold Cup. The fittest of the five fastest horses is awarded the Austin-Carroll Trophy. Buckles are awarded for all horses finishing fit in a riding time of 21 hours or less. In 1978 41 competitors started; 28 'successfully completed the ride'. For results see Appendix 2.

12

Many endurance rides are now organized in Australia, principally in New South Wales, Queensland and Victoria.

South Africa   The principle ride is the National Endurance Ride, which prior to 1977 was called the Arabian Horse Floating Trophy Endurance Ride. The total distance covered is 131 miles (210 km) split 50-50-31 (80-80-50) between three consecutive days. The route is hilly. The weather is variable; the temperature may be down to freezing or up in the eighties (over 25°C); hot sunshine may alternate with driving rain. The two 50 mile circuits are divided by one 1 hour and one $\frac{1}{2}$ hour halt, and the 31 miles by one $\frac{1}{2}$ hour halt. Horses, unless their riders are under sixteen, must carry 161 lbs (73 kg) minimum. They must be not less than $4\frac{1}{2}$ years old. Pregnant mares are banned. Spurs are not allowed, whips must not be more than 27 inches (68 cm) long. Hard hats are compulsory. The horse finishing in the fastest time and satisfying the veterinary team is awarded the *Farmer's Weekly* Floating Trophy; the horse finishing in the best condition among the fastest ten, the Arabian Horse Floating Trophy. Of those which complete the 131 miles within 20 hours riding time the faster half are awarded buckles and the rest certificates of achievement. For results see Appendix 3.

Britain   Here no named ride has established itself as the leading annual event. In fact Britain had no endurance rides, in the strict sense of the term, between 1921 and 1973, the year when the Endurance Horse and Pony Society was founded. In 1975 this society organized the first one day 100 mile (160 km) ride ever run in Britain — The Summer Solstice. A further one day 100 mile ride followed two years later, but, not being run at mid-summer, it could not keep the name. For 1978 two rides were listed, one 50 miles and one 60 (80 and 76 km).

Long Distance Races

These are uncommon. This is principally because, since the winner is not required to finish in 'fit condition to continue', other and more awkward precautions must be taken against the possibility of horses being over ridden. This danger can only be avoided by restricting entries to riders who have proved sufficiently knowledgeable to be able to look after their mounts during the race, and sufficiently humane to value their well-being, even in the heat of the moment, more highly than victory. In these circumstances, deciding which entries to accept and which to reject is both difficult and invidious.

In Britain the Arab Horse Society has run its $26\frac{1}{4}$ mile (42 km) Marathon Race annually since 1974. Weight carried is 161 lbs (73 kg). On all but one occasion it has proved possible to start the whole field together so that the first horse past the post could also be the winner. The course includes compulsory walking sections, totalling roughly a mile (1·6 km), but no halts. Veterinary supervision consists in inspection before the race, observation of the field from various points along the route with full power to eliminate and inspection both at the finish and again after a lapse of half an hour. No horse would be placed if the veterinary team considered him to have been ill-used, but minor unsoundnesses, which would temporarily prevent his further use, are not causes for disqualification. Encouraging and reassuring information about the subsequent history of the Marathon horses has been diligently collected.

Ride and Tie Races

These are the invention of Mr Bud Johns, Levi Strauss and Co's publicity officer in the United States, inspired by reading that in earlier times, when two people with only one horse between them wanted to get somewhere in a hurry, one rode a convenient distance, dismounted, tied up the horse and ran on, while the other ran to where the horse was tied, mounted and rode till he had outdistanced his companion, dismounted, tied up the horse and so on. Mr Johns' inspiration bore fruit in the Levi Ride and Tie Race, run annually since 1971.

The course chosen for this race is not always the same and its length has varied from 28 to 38·9 miles (45-62·6 km). This

14

Riders and runners at the start of the 1975 Levi Ride and Tie. (USA)

last was covered by the 1977 winning team in 4 hours 18 minutes 20 seconds — that is at an average speed of 9·03 mph (14·53 kph). Competitors start simultaneously, riders and runners spread out over a wide front (see photo above). A team finishes when the last of its members crosses the finishing line.

Ride and Tie races are not for unknowledgeable or careless riders, still less for inexperienced organizers. The horses must stand tied up and unattended (not permitted at all on most endurance rides), and for this they must have the right temperament and be well trained. They have to stand immediately after fast work, so that they easily become chilled unless great care is taken. The rules of the Levi Ride and Tie provide for veterinary inspection before and after the race and at a number of compulsory tieing points. In 1975, for instance, on a course of 30 miles (48 km), there were five compulsory tieing points at 5, 11, 17, 22 and 24 miles (8, 17·6, 27·3, 35·5 and 38·6 km). At the first, second and fourth horses were examined by a vet and required to remain for a fixed resting period; at the others they were permitted to leave after simply having been looked at.

Veterinarians have power to eliminate a horse or to order him to rest for up to an hour. All horses, whether they have completed the course or been voluntarily or compulsorily withdrawn, are examined again one hour after the race has ended. Compulsory ties apart, a team may tie its horse when, where and for as long as it pleases.

There are few Ride and Tie races anywhere. As yet none have been run in Britain, though one is now being planned. The Levi Ride and Tie itself is deservedly popular, both with competitors and with spectators. In 1974 it was watched by more than 10,000 people. Many teams compete not to win but to complete the course — in itself a considerable feat. Human partners are often members of one family. Ride and Tie Buckles are highly valued. Ride and Tie racing, responsibly organized, is one of the most rewarding and exciting forms of the long distance sport.

Type B

We have divided long distance rides in which speed is not the only criterion of success, into Trials and Tests. These words once commonly appeared in the titles of rides but without any precise meaning; today they no longer form part of the long distance riding vocabulary at all. But they aptly distinguish the two categories of rides for which we have used them, categories which are fundamentally different but which for historical and geographical reasons have never so far been named.

Long Distance Trials

In these, horses are placed in an order commensurate with the merit of their *total* performance. They are therefore judged according to both the time they take to complete the course and the ease with which they complete it. The criteria used to evaluate these two aspects of performance vary greatly.

Today nearly all trials are of a particular kind devized in the United States and called Competitive Trail Rides. These differ

Tevis Cup: approaching Cougar Rock. (USA)

Tevis Cup: cooling off in Eldorado River in the bottom of the canyons. (USA)

Tevis Cup: the bottom of the canyons. (USA)

from other trials in that the time rewarded is not a fast time, but an exact time: a horse which performs perfectly goes, like a train running to schedule, fast enough not to arrive at his destination late, but never so fast that he arrives early.

In the United States itself a competitive trail ride may occupy one, two or three days. If one day, then the distance ridden is at least 30 miles (48 km); if two, then 50 miles (80 km) divided into 25 and 25 (40 and 40); if three, then 100 miles (160 km) divided into 40, 40 and 20 (25, 25 and 32 km). A distance of 40 miles must usually be travelled in between 6 and 7 hours — that is, at an average speed of between 6·66 and 5·71 mph (10·7-9·1 kph). The degree of importance attached to speed varies slightly from one ride to another. Thus some penalize a competitor's failure to finish within the fixed time interval by elimination, others only by deducting points from his total score (usually one for every three minutes or part of three minutes that he is late or early), while yet others compromise and deduct points until his accumulated lateness from day to day reaches one hour, when he is eliminated.

It is important to note that the average speeds within which a competitor is required to complete a course are overall speeds, not riding speeds. A prospective competitor must, therefore, find out how much time he is compelled to lose at halts and from this work out how much will be left for actual riding.

The ease with which a horse performs is scored under several headings. The North American Trail Ride Conference advocates marking by a system which assumes perfection equal to 100 and then deducts penalty points as follows: for unsoundness up to 40; for less than perfect 'condition' up to 40; for 'way of going' up to 5; and for defective manners up to 15.

Judgment of condition is based on observations made at halts during the ride — these are more numerous than in endurance rides — after the ride and, sometimes, on the following day.

Because part of the object of a competitive trail ride is to reward the ease with which a horse completes the course, the use of 'artificial aids' is banned. These, by helping to make good the deficiencies of some horses, would falsify the results. Thus the North American Trail Ride Conference prohibits the use of stimulants, anti-inflammatory drugs and pain killers, bandages and guards, hoof pads, liniments, alcohol and ice. For the same reason it does not allow a rider to help his horse by walking or running any part of the way.

Competitive trail rides in the United States are often combined with horsemanship competitions. These do not require a further performance by horse and rider; the two competitions are run concurrently and judged separately. Horsemanship points are awarded for: presentation of horse, correct fitting of saddlery, care bestowed on the horse at stops, the hands and seat of the rider and the rider's general sportsmanship and consideration for other people.

Competitive trail rides have not so far become popular in Australia, and none are organized in the main trail riding areas which border the east coast.

In Britain these were introduced by the Endurance Horse and Pony Society and none have so far been organized by any other body. Distances vary between 25 and 60 miles (40-96 km). Rides are divided into 'ordinary' and 'fast'. For the first the average speed required for a perfect time score is one between 6 and 7 mph (9-11 kph) one penalty point being deducted for every three minutes by which a horse's speed is too fast or too slow. However, mere deduction of points is the penalty only so long as a horse's speed is too fast or too slow by up to 1 mph (1·6 kph); if he averages more than 8 mph (13 kph) or less than 6 (9 km), he is disqualified. Fast rides are run over shorter distances. For these the perfect speed is set as one between 8 and 9 mph (13-14·6 kph), a horse being disqualified if he goes slower than 7 mph (11 kph) or faster than 10 (16 km). The E.H.P.S. system of judging a competitor's performance on counts other than timing is simpler than that normally used in the United States. Only veterinary surgeons judge and they are asked simply to place the horses in an order commensurate with the condition they have shown during and after the ride. In neither country do the rules permit dead heats. If two horses

Midnight: the start of the first Quilty, 1966. (Australia)

happen to be given the same marks, they are sent out again to travel a further distance and re-judged when they return.

Long Distance Trials of a different kind were organized in Britain a few years ago by the Arab Horse Society. In these the time rewarded was fast time and not exact time.

Long distance tests

Rides of this kind are at present almost entirely confined to Britain, though there is some indication that they may now spread to the continent of Europe. The British Horse Society is responsible for the important Golden Horseshoe Ride, which is spread over two days, 50 miles (80 km) being ridden on the first day and 25 (40 km) on the second. Four standards of achievement, each demanding different combinations of time and veterinary marks, are rewarded with four classes of award: Golden Horseshoes, Silver Horseshoes, Bronze Horseshoes and Rosettes. As the system of marking is at present being revised, it would be misleading to describe it in detail. Other tests, which are qualifiers for the Golden Horseshoe Ride, are also organized by this society.

Rides without an overall winner are unknown in Australia and the United States. There is, however, some justification for saying that endurance rides are ridden as tests by those whose sole aim is to arrive at the end of the course fit and within the maximum time allowed. All buckles are equal in value, and it is the buckle, not the placing, which counts for the Tevis or Quilty competitor who finishes in, for instance, 30th or 40th place.

Type C

Non-competitive rides

These are usually called pleasure rides. They cover 15 miles (24 km) or more. Although they are normally ridden purely for the joy of riding through open country, those who complete them within a certain time are sometimes awarded rosettes.

It might be thought that this kind of riding would require no organization, but some people prefer to ride in company and along a route which has been planned for them. Moreover in Britain an organization often obtains permission to ride over private land more easily than an individual.

In the United States and Australia pleasure riding is closely associated with the attempt to keep the old trails open. In 1972 the Australian Trail Horse Riders Association was formed specifically for this purpose. This Association and its affiliated clubs are dedicated to 'the establishment of a continuous trail along the eastern edge of Australia, from Melbourne to Cooktown' — some 1900 miles (3057 km).

2 A suitable horse

Any horse, given some training, can be used for the shorter pleasure rides. A considerable variety of horses, given good training, can be used for trials, tests and pleasure rides of medium length and difficulty. But for endurance rides, for races, for longer trials where the competition is strong and for tests where the standard is high, a really suitable and very well trained horse is necessary. On most of these rides the horse will have to travel over difficult country and will have to travel continuously for a long time without unduly tiring either himself or his rider. He needs, therefore, to be constructed in such a way that he moves easily; he needs to be physically able to produce the power to keep himself moving and his temperament needs to be such that he has both the will to go and the sense not to waste energy. It is convenient to discuss this horse under 'Ease of movement', 'Power of movement', 'Temperament'.

Ease of movement

A horse which moves easily is, on the whole, one which has correct riding conformation. But the long distance horse is not a show horse and for him some good conformational points are much more important than others. The show horse does well enough if he moves easily for a short time over flat, level and resilient ground; the long distance horse only does well if he moves easily for a very long time over ground which is often hilly, rough and either hard or holding. He needs, therefore, to be particularly strong in the following respects.

Point of balance This should be as far back as possible. A horse's shoulder, upper arm and forearm have only to swing

23

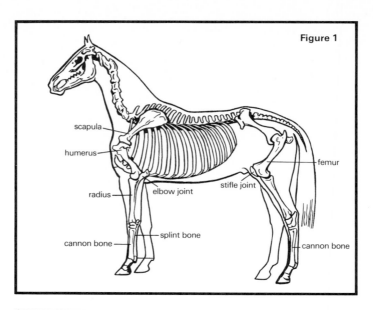

Figure 1

scapula

humerus

radius

elbow joint

cannon bone

splint bone

femur

stifle joint

cannon bone

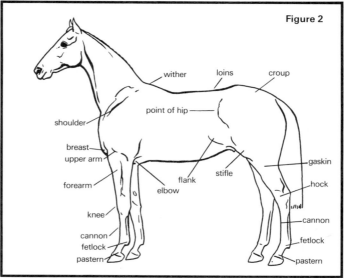

Figure 2

wither   loins   croup

point of hip

shoulder

breast
upper arm

forearm

flank   stifle

elbow

gaskin

hock

knee

cannon
fetlock
pastern

cannon

fetlock

pastern

24

themselves forward; it is his hind quarters which provide the propulsion, while muscles in his back lift his forehand clear of the ground. How easily this last can be done depends on the weight to be lifted. All horses are heavier in front than behind — the point of balance can never be further back than their middle — but some are much heavier in front than others. Lightness on the forehand is the first essential for ease of movement and economy of energy. Thus the long distance horse needs a light head and his neck must never be heavily muscled, although it must be reasonably long to allow him to keep his balance over rough going and up and down hill. Even his forelegs should be on the light side; dense bone is desirable, but any advantage gained from the strength of a great circumference of bone below the knee and heavy muscling of the forearm is more than offset by the accompanying increase in weight. Above all, the breast must not be wide; width here is no indication of room for heart and lungs and as well as adding unnecessary weight it greatly reduces agility.

Length of stride   The fewer the number of strides a horse takes to reach the end of a course the better, for three reasons. First, fewer strides put less total strain on his legs — each time a foot hits the ground the resulting concussion jars the leg above it, and continuously repeated jarring, particularly at a fast trot, eventually damages ligaments and tendons. Secondly, fewer strides require less energy — compare a slowly walking adult with a small child running to keep up with him. Thirdly, long strides are less tiring for the rider.

The length of a horse's stride can be increased by schooling, but only if he already has the right conformation. To stride out in front he needs a long shoulder (scapula) and one which slopes at an angle of 45°, or slightly more, in relation to the ground; a short and rather upright upper arm (humerus), a long forearm; a short cannon and a moderately long pastern which repeats the angle of his shoulder. To follow through well behind, he needs a femur also angled at 45° or slightly more, a hind leg long from stifle to hock and short from hock to fetlock, and moderately long pasterns, which may be at a slightly steeper angle than those in front. Most of these conformational qualities can be judged at a glance by noticing whether a horse is 'standing over a lot of ground', that is to say, whether, when he is standing up well and his hocks are not out behind him, the distance between his front and hind foot is long in proportion to the distance between the top of his shoulder and his quarters.

Balance and rhythm   If a horse does not move with balance and rhythm, he tires quickly. Learning to move in this way forms the major part of his early schooling, but here again a suitable conformation is necessary. He requires all the characteristics listed under the two previous headings and, in addition, a head well set on to his neck, a neck well set on to his body, elbow and stifle joints well clear of chest and flank and legs which are free from the malformations discussed below.

Ability to move without incurring injury   Some horses have a tendency to hit one limb with another — to interfere. Many which never interfere on rides of normal length begin to do so as they tire towards the end of a long ride. Interference is particularly likely when the limbs in front and behind slope inwards so that they are nearer together at the bottom than the top — when they are what is called in the United States 'base narrow'. The likelihood is greatly increased when in addition the feet turn out, and to some extent even when they turn in. But not all horses with these conformational defects in fact injure themselves, even after they have been ridden a very long way. Horses can also interfere by hitting a front leg with a hind foot or a hind leg with a front foot when galloping (speedy cutting), or by hitting a hind cannon with a front foot (scalping) when trotting, or the sole or heel of a front foot with the toe of a hind when trotting or walking (forging and overreaching). The latter can result in the loss of a front shoe. Although for success in the showring a horse must travel on two tracks, keeping his hind feet precisely in line with his front ones, all danger of

26

Tevis Cup: horse and rider resting and cooling part way up the canyons. (USA)

Tevis Cup: crossing a bridge in the canyons. (USA)

Above The Arab gelding El Ganat competing in the San Antonio 50 mile (80 km) Endurance Ride at the age of 20. He completed the Tevis when he was 18 and again when he was 19. (USA)

Above right The Quilty begins at midnight. A rider in the dark. (Australia)

Below right The Quilty: many miles of the route are over steep and rocky track. (Australia)

Shalawi, Arab stallion, passing the finishing post to win the first Quilty. He was ridden the entire distance without a saddle. (Australia)

Shalawi grazing unconcernedly immediately after his win. (Australia)

interference between hind and front legs is avoided if, instead, he places his hind feet outside the line of his front ones; a few successful long distance horses have moved in this way, though it is ungainly to look at and not particularly comfortable for the rider.

A horse's legs are more likely to be damaged by concussion when the angles of shoulder, femur and pasterns are steeper than those described above, since a leg which is over straight (when seen from the side) has little spring. The longer the pasterns, the greater the spring, but the greater also the strain on tendons and ligaments. Riders do not agree on ideal pastern length. (When seen from the front the foreleg must, of course, always be straight, that is at right angles to the ground, from elbow to fetlock, and the hind leg straight from hock to fetlock.)

Concussion is also absorbed by the frog in the foot; this must be well developed and in contact with the ground whenever the foot is bearing weight. Small feet are a serious disadvantage; principally because they provide too small a weight-carrying area and too small a frog. But disproportionately large feet make a horse clumsy and apt to stumble.

Good joints, including large, flat knees and large hocks, and good tendons are also necessary to guard against injury.

However, not all irregularities in leg conformation in fact lead to the damage which might be expected. It is true that pronounced sickle hocks, always a weakness and said to predispose to curbs, should be avoided. We have already mentioned that a horse which is base narrow, splay-footed or pigeon-toed will be liable to interfere. These faults also cause the affected legs to bear weight incorrectly. But the apparently predictable damage does not always follow. Nor have cow hocks (hocks turned in) invariably proved a handicap. These are penalized in the showring and some people believe they predispose to spavin. But in fact many very successful long distance horses have been cow hocked. Offset cannons (bench knees in the USA) are another fault usually regarded as serious but which occur in top class long distance performers. (A horse has an offset cannon when the radius above the knee and the

31

Severe sickle hocks: sickle hocks are not to be confused with hocks out behind. This horse's point of hock is correctly in line with his point of buttock but below the hock the leg slopes under him. A curb was already forming when the photograph as taken (arrow); after he started work it developed further and he became lame.

cannon bone below it are out of line with one another, although at right angles to the ground.) It is essential that horses with this conformational defect should not be worked when young; given time, the splint bone usually develops sufficiently to bear the additional strain.

Ability to carry a saddle The horse which carries a saddle well is not humpy (roach) backed and although his back must not actually be hollow, there must be a slight dip behind his withers where the saddle can fit comfortably. The saddle must also stay put without the girths being excessively tight; if the horse has a moderately high wither with some muscling, then it will not slip forwards; if he has well sprung ribs, it will not slip back; and if his elbow is well forward (as it will be if his shoulder is long and sloping and his upper arm fairly straight) and not tucked in to his chest, then there will be plenty of room for the girth so that it will not chafe or cause sores and galls.

Ability to carry a rider Some horses are often more tired at the end of a long ride when they have been ridden slowly than when they have been ridden fast, simply because they have carried the rider's weight for a longer time. This shows the importance of the right conformation for carrying weight — a short, strong back. So, in choosing a horse the rider should look for one which is well ribbed up, that is, with only a small gap between the end of his ribs and his point of hip, and level and well muscled over his loins.

Power of movement

A horse moves when his muscles contract and expand; to do this they need energy. Energy is produced in the muscles from fuel (muscular substrate) which consists of carbohydrates, proteins and fats. Some of this fuel is synthesized from food which the horse has recently eaten, some is drawn from reserves stored in the liver and in the muscles themselves; only when these sources are depleted is energy output maintained from fuel which has been stored as body fat.

Parts of the processes whereby energy is derived from muscular fuels require oxygen. This, like the fuel itself, is carried to the muscles by the blood which has been replenished with oxygen on its circuit through the lungs — the lungs themselves having obtained oxygen from the outer air as the horse breathed in. The production of energy in the muscles gives rise to carbon dioxide as a waste product. This is carried back to the lungs by the blood and thence breathed out. The blood is pumped by the heart through the muscles on one circuit and through the lungs on another. The release of energy in the muscles also generates heat, so the blood leaves the muscles hot. The blood cools as it passes close to the surface of the skin and the surface of the lungs when these are filled with cooler air. We shall have more to say about heat in Chapter 5.

From all this it is clear that a horse's power of movement depends primarily on the efficiency of his skeletal muscles, of his lungs and their accompanying air passages (his respiratory system), of his heart and its accompanying blood vessels (his cardio-vascular system) and of his digestion. (It also depends on his brain and less directly on other aspects of his physical make-up and his physiology.)

Witezarif, Arab gelding, and Donna Fitzgerald, who together have won the Tevis Cup five times and tied for it once. (USA)

Efficiency of muscles   Since it is the muscles which directly move the limbs, it is important for the horse to be well muscled. The building up of muscle is one of the main purposes of training. But there remains the question, 'What kind of muscles and where?' Long muscles contract and expand further than short muscles. Long leg muscles move the limbs which they control further with each expansion and contraction and are therefore essential for long strides. But these muscles can also be either flat or what is variously described as heavy, thick, bulky or bunchy. Bulky muscles are more powerful than flat muscles — they can contract and expand more quickly and so allow a horse (or a man) to travel faster even though he may be taking shorter strides. They are, however, unable to go on contracting and expanding for any length of time. Thus, on a race course the bulkily muscled sprinter is fast up to 6 furlongs (1·2 km) but is easily overtaken by the flat muscled stayer at a mile or a mile and a half (2·4 km). The reason for this appears to be that

34

thick muscles are more difficult than flat ones for the blood to service; perhaps more difficult for it to keep supplied with oxygen and certainly more difficult for it to cool, since a smaller proportion of their total volume is near the skin. Thus the muscles which move the horse's legs must be both long and flat.

In considering a young horse for future training it is not always easy to judge what his muscles will be like when they have developed. Length of muscle is easier to forecast than flatness since it is always proportionate to skeletal frame. Flatness of muscle, though also related to frame and certainly influenced by heredity, is hard to forecast with accuracy. New research into muscle structure has shown that different types of muscle are composed of different proportions of three separate kinds of muscle fibre. Samples of muscle can now be taken for examination with a specially designed needle. In 1976 Mr Peter Rossdale, in his book *Inside the Horse*, was able to write: 'As more information becomes available, we might be able to classify foals, predicting their probable distance and even their athletic performance.'

The long distance horse needs well developed muscles in his hindquarters and his back and sufficient muscling on the forehand to swing his front legs well forward and maintain his balance. But superfluous muscling is a handicap; it adds weight and, because it increases his volume in relation to his body surface, makes it more difficult for him to keep cool.

Efficiency of lungs and air passages The amount of oxygen which the blood can collect from the lungs to carry to the muscles depends partly on how much air is drawn in with each breath, and partly on the size of the area within the lungs over which the blood comes so near to the air that it can exchange its old gasses for new — carbon dioxide for oxygen. Mr Rossdale has vividly pointed out that in each lung this area is almost the size of a tennis court.

Lung function also can be improved by training; a fit horse is able to expand his chest farther than an unfit one, so that his lungs also expand farther and take in more air. But here too the success of the training depends on the raw material the trainer has to work with. It is a firmly established belief that unless a horse has had a good gallop in the first few days of his life, his lungs can never be fully expanded. It is also necessary that the whole area of both 'tennis courts' should be available for full use; that is, that every part of the area over which oxygen and carbon dioxide can be exchanged should be clear and undamaged by past infections or fungi breathed in from mouldy hay. Hay is more often mouldy than the inexperienced horseman would suppose.

The passages through which the air reaches the lungs must be roomy and free from obstruction. The horse needs large and easily expanded nostrils and plenty of room for his larynx and windpipe where his head joins his neck.

Efficiency of heart   An efficient heart beats slowly. It does so because it is able to pump a large quantity of blood with each beat, and so has no need to beat fast. If one horse's heart beats more slowly than another's when he is resting, it will also beat more slowly when he is trotting and galloping; so that at every level of activity his heart will need to work less hard and will be subjected to less strain, and he will also be able to work at a level at which the second horse cannot work at all.

A slow beating heart is more useful to the long distance horse than any other single asset; thus most serious long distance riders choose a horse with a slow resting pulse rate. Heart speed is measured in beats per minute. Sometimes this measurement is taken directly by listening to the horse's heart with a stethoscope and counting the beats, and sometimes indirectly by feeling the blood pulsing through a conveniently sited artery and counting the pulse beats; for this reason it is sometimes referred to as 'heart rate' and sometimes 'pulse rate'. Pulse rate is the term always used in long distance riding; in ride rules, on vetting cards and in ride results.

The true resting pulse rate of a horse is difficult to establish accurately, since it is impossible to gauge the extent to which he is really resting. Dr C. B. Throgmorton in his paper *Inter-*

pretation of Pulse and Respiration has written that when a horse is resting completely the pulse varies between 28 and 40 beats per minute; but he points out that horses rarely are resting completely when their pulses are taken, so he coins the term 'normally aroused' and gives the pulse rate of a normally aroused horse as between 32 and 48. He adds the interesting information that at one pre-Tevis Ride inspection pulse rates varied between 36 and 60. Mr Rossdale states (*Inside the Horse*) that the resting pulse rate of an adult horse is in the region of 40 beats per minute, of a yearling in the region of 60 and of a foal in the region of 80. An owner can often establish the resting pulse rate of a horse which knows him well with a fair degree of accuracy, since he may be able to take his pulse when he is lying down and he can certainly take it often and average the results. But an intending buyer will be unable to make any useful comparison between the resting pulse rates of two horses taken only on one occasion and in unspecified or different conditions. Moreover, since even a resting pulse rate is to some extent lowered by training, it would be necessary to make allowance for their relative fitness. Resting pulse rates of foals and young horses, which tend to be more excitable than adults, are normally more difficult to establish.

The alternative method of judging the efficiency of a horse's heart is by estimating its size. Large hearts, not surprisingly, can pump more blood per beat than small ones. Big hearts have always been considered an advantage on the race course. Some Thoroughbreds' hearts have weighed as little as 5 lb (2·2 kg), but Eclipse's scaled 14 lb (6·3 kg) and Phar Lap's $13\frac{1}{2}$ (6·1 kg). However, until recently it has been difficult to use this criterion, since it has been impossible to establish heart size in a living horse. The best that a rider could do was to choose a horse which might have a big heart because his deep chest allowed sufficient room. However, it is now already more than a decade since the late Professor Steele of Melbourne University established a correlation between heart size and certain electrocardiograph measurements. This has provided a new and most valuable tool for predicting at any age how a horse will later perform over a long distance course — a tool which Australian riders, particularly those who breed their own horses, have been quick to adopt.

Efficiency of digestion In Britain and Australia a horse with a good digestion is called a 'good doer'; in the United States he is said to have 'good keeping quality'. Such an animal makes the best use of what he eats and so needs comparatively little food; he has a good appetite and so can be fed a wide variety of feeding stuffs; he is not easily perturbed, so he does not lose his appetite away from home and he is not subject to digestive upsets and colic. Whether a young horse not being fed concentrated food has such a digestion, it is difficult to tell. How well he looks on the food he is currently being fed gives some indication. No horse will do well unless his teeth are in good order, and this at least can be ascertained.

Temperament

A horse is of no use for long distance unless he is keen to go and still has some keenness left right through to the end. On the other hand he must be a sensible horse; sufficiently placid to be unaffected by unusual happenings and surroundings, so that his normal pattern of eating, sleeping and resting is undisturbed.

Age, height, sex and breed

Age Most riders agree that horses under 5 years old are insufficiently mature; they also agree that by the time a horse is 14 or 15 he is usually past his best; but horses have still performed well at 16 and 17; occasionally a 19 or 20 year old has completed, even won, a 100 mile (160 km) endurance ride.

Height It would be natural to suppose that, providing a horse has the right proportions, the bigger the better; for, being bigger in relation to his rider, he should be able to carry him more easily and, being bigger in relation to the distance he has

Shareym, Arab stallion, who completed six Quilties, the last when he was 16.
He is seen here in unfit condition. (Australia)

Shareym in training fit to take part in a long distance ride. (Australia)

Unregistered mare, Cindy, winner of the 1970 Quilty, at the pre-ride examination. (Australia)

to cover, he should reach the end of the course in fewer strides and with a smaller expenditure of energy. In fact nearly all the best long distance horses have measured about 15 hands (152 cms). Few 16 hand (162 cms) horses have proved satisfactory, even those belonging to the most successful breeds.

Sex   Most of the horses now used are geldings; some are mares, but only a few stallions. This would have seemed surprising to pre-World War II long distance riders. They believed that the courage and spirit of a stallion made him more suitable than a mare or gelding. Modern riders consider that this advantage is more than outweighed by his tendency to waste energy and his frequent failure to rest. It is significant that, though the first two Tevis Cups were won by stallions and the third by a mare, 16 out of the last 20 have been won by geldings and that in 1977 geldings took the first nineteen places, no stallion being placed higher than fortieth. (It should perhaps be noted that before World War II few suitable horses were gelded in countries where long distance rides were held.)

Breed   In the United States and Britain the great majority of successful horses have always been Arabs or near Arabs. Many important events in Australia have been won by Australian stock horses whose pedigrees often reveal Arab breeding.

Health

A horse in all other respects eminently suitable must still be rejected if past ill-health or accident have left him in any way permanently incapacitated. We have already mentioned lung damage resulting from respiratory disease or mouldy hay; but he may also have been harmed by other diseases, by worm infestation, by under or over feeding, by being ridden too young, by bad shoeing, by careless saddling, by general mismanagement or by injury. It is easier for a rider to assess the permanence and seriousness of such damage if he has known the horse for some time or is familiar with his history.

3 How should a horse be trained?

It is best if a rider trains his horse himself, since only by so doing can he become sufficiently familiar with his behaviour to interpret it correctly; to recognize, for instance, when he is in fact very tired, although to someone who knew him less well he might appear still full of going. This arrangement also increases the rider's own fitness and it accustoms the horse to the way in which he will be ridden on the ride.

In this chapter we shall assume that the horse to be trained has already undergone a thorough elementary schooling, when he will have learnt to move freely under saddle. Although some horses receive this initial instruction in the process of becoming stock horses, most are schooled in a more formal way. Many books are available on this subject; it is convenient to begin here at the point when, having learnt his preliminary lessons well and been turned out for two or three weeks' rest he is ready to start his training for long distance. He must now a) be taught how to negotiate ride country with a minimum expenditure of energy, b) be made sufficiently fit for the ride or rides in which his owner intends him to compete and c) be taught how to behave in a relaxed and unperturbed manner in the conditions which surround a long distance ride.

The accomplishments a horse learns under headings a) and c) he learns once and for all — though if he is unworked for a while, he may well need a refresher course. The speed with which he learns them depends on his conformation and on his temperament. But acquiring fitness is altogether different. During a long rest a horse loses his fitness and at the end of it his training must start all over again. How long it takes to make the horse fit will depend partly on how long he has been rested and partly on the length and severity of the rides in which he will be asked to compete. A good horse brought in from a fortnight's rest, which has followed immediately upon his schooling, can be made fit enough to go 100 miles (160 km) in 3 months; but a horse schooled sometime previously and beginning his long distance training in a totally unfit state will need 6 months or more. The fact that a horse is relatively quickly trained for short rides must not blind us to the fact that thorough training is necessary for every level of competition. Mishaps occur all too easily whenever a horse is asked to go further or faster than his current condition warrants.

Teaching a horse to negotiate ride country

A horse with the right conformation, well schooled, will move without wasting energy in the schooling area itself and out on a casual hack. But further skills and experience are needed if he is not to make clumsy and unnecessary movements, or to become tense or hesitant, in the kind of country and on the kinds of route which are common on long distance rides. For many he must learn the most economical way of going up and down hill and gain experience in winding his way along narrow hillside tracks. For all he will have to become familiar with one or more of the less favourable forms of going: tarred roads, hard rock, soft sand or bog, ground covered by loose stones or flints or hidden under thick vegetation. On most he will have to wade through water and on some even to swim. For 100 mile (160 km) rides, which take the greater part of 24 hours, he must acquire the ability to move with as much confidence in the dark as in the daylight. He must also form the habit of trotting and cantering in a relaxed and carefree manner wherever good going makes it unnecessary for him to hold himself alert against the danger of a false step. The negotiation of hills requires further discussion.

Travelling downhill

What method is chosen to travel downhill is always important and often crucial. On rides with a significant downhill mileage

Tailing on the Tevis. (USA)

Bright Hope, Anglo-Arab mare, and Minette Rice-Edwards at Cougar Rock on the 1973 Tevis where they won the Haggin Cup. Although riding up this hill Mrs Rice-Edwards tailed up many, and ran and walked a total of 15 miles (24 km). (USA)

44

(number of kilometres) it may make the difference between failure and success (it will be remembered from Chapter 1 that the Tevis route falls by 15,000 ft (4572 m) and the Quilty by over 10,000 (3048)).

In Britain, where few riders have experience of long and difficult routes, it is often believed that if a hill is steep then the rider should dismount at the top and walk, or possibly jog, down with his horse keeping pace behind him as best he can. But in Australia and the United States riders agree that the proper speed for going down hills is a fast one, particularly on endurance rides, for three reasons. First, facing downhill, even when standing still, is very tiring for the muscles of a horse's hind quarters, thus the less time he has to spend in this position the better. Secondly, it is in fact, more difficult and more tiring for him to go slowly than fast. For here it is gravity that provides the greater part of the power; he moves his legs not so much to go forward as to remain balanced. Thus he uses less energy for the whole descent (though not, of course, per stride) by allowing himself to be carried forward at a fast speed than by holding himself back to a slow one. Thirdly, on an endurance ride, where the speed averaged over the whole course must be fast, the rider must make the best use of all stretches where the horse can travel fastest with the least expenditure of energy; these are downhill.

There is, however, one disadvantage to fast downhill travel: the strain it places on tendons and ligaments. With the force of gravity behind him a horse's feet hit the ground harder than they do on the flat; they also hit it at an awkward angle.

The great majority of riders think that the best pace downhill is a trot, only a few prefer a canter and a very few, who are sufficiently athletic to run without getting in their horse's way, so breaking his rhythm, choose to descend dismounted.

Trotting fast downhill is something no horse does naturally, and a few cannot learn at all. Most break into a canter and try to race when their training begins; they must be pulled up and put quietly at the slope again. Gentle gradients should be used in the early stages and steeper ones introduced gradually as the horse becomes increasingly able to trot out fast, stretching his forelegs well out in front and bringing his hind legs well in beneath him. The hills chosen should have good going: moderately soft, not slippery and free from stones, but if a horse is likely to meet bad downhill going on a ride then he must be permitted some experience of it beforehand. This skill once learnt is never forgotten. Since the movement requires a unique kind of muscular activity, the horse must practice if he is to move in this way on a ride without ill effect, but excessive practice puts unnecessary strain on tendons and ligaments.

Travelling uphill

Uphill, gravity is against the horse. Climbing requires much energy, so long or steep hills should be climbed slowly. Experience has shown that for rides with considerable uphill mileage the method of climbing known as 'tailing' can be used with great advantage.* The rider dismounts; if he is wise, he ties a thin line to the bridle; he then sends the horse ahead and goes up holding on to his tail. (This is not of course possible on competitive trail rides where the rule is that a rider may not 'proceed' unmounted.) The virtues of tailing are that the horse is able to climb freed of the rider's weight and unhindered by his walking in front of him or at his side, while the rider goes up much more easily, with the pull afforded by the grip on the horse's tail, than he would if he had to provide the necessary energy himself. Few riders would find it physically possible to climb some hills as fast as a horse does, or indeed, on a ride like the Tevis, to climb all the necessary hills at all. (But it is interesting to note that in 1974 Gordy Ainsleigh, who had already ridden one Tevis, made history by running the course on foot; his time being 23 hours 42 minutes. 1978 saw the first 100 mile (160 km) Western States Endurance Run over the Tevis course. Out of the 69 entries, 16 completed the course within 24 hours, and a further 12 within 30 hours. Andy Gonzales, the winner, set up a remarkable record with a time of 18 hours 50 minutes.)

* At the present time this method is practised in the United States and South Africa but not in Australia.

It is not difficult to teach a horse to tail. The rider begins by pulling on his tail when grooming him, and making him thoroughly used to his presence close behind, and then goes on to holding his tail when walking. Surprisingly few horses mind.

Making a horse fit

In the United States this aspect of a horse's training is called 'conditioning'. In Britain we do not yet speak of 'conditioning' a horse and it would be confusing for us to do so, since 'improving a horse's condition' normally means increasing his weight, which is not conducive to fitness. But we are badly in need of a term. There is no verb 'to fitten', the purists dislike the common expression 'to get fit', while 'to train' and 'to prepare' have wider meanings. 'Make fit' seems the least objectionable alternative, but we shall also use the word 'train' and its derivatives in contexts where the meaning intended is plain.

Making a horse fit consists in increasing his power to move, as opposed to improving the manner in which he moves. His power to move can only be increased by exercise.

If a horse is repeatedly worked somewhat harder (not longer) than it is easy for him to work, his power will increase until the work once difficult becomes easy. This fact provides the basis for planning a horse's exercise. As soon as he finds work at one level easy, he is asked to work harder and when that too becomes easy, harder again. His training proceeds in this fashion until either he is sufficiently fit for the rides in which his owner wishes to compete or until a demand is made to which he fails to respond. Such failure indicates that he is now as fit as he will ever be; further training is then both harmful and futile. If this degree of fitness is insufficient for his rider's requirements, the latter will have to look for another horse.

Judging a horse's fitness
A rider must be able to assess his horse's improvement. Only then can he decide whether he needs more work and when he

47

needs a rest. Skeletal muscles which are unfit look formless and feel soft or fleshy, so their increasing fitness can in part be judged by look and feel. But the fitness of heart and lungs must be judged by how well they work. This, in the past, a rider estimated entirely from observing his horse at work; timing him over a distance, feeling what he was like to ride, noticing what he looked like and how he behaved later. He noted among other things, his keenness to go, the extent to which he puffed and blew at the end of a gallop and how profusely he sweated. Today, though long distance riders still take all these observations into account, they consider that the most reliable guide to his degree of fitness is how quickly his pulse drops back to near normal after work.

The pulse rate, as we saw in the last chapter, rises as the horse exerts himself. The fitter he is, the less far it will rise with a given degree of exertion, and the faster it will fall back to normal when the exertion ceases. Because the rate immediately a horse stops trotting, galloping or climbing is very greatly affected by his speed immediately before he stopped, it is not, by itself, significant. It is how far and how fast it falls that gives a clear indication of the ease with which he has performed his task. Thus, if on two occasions a horse is worked over the same ground, in the same time and in similar weather and other conditions, the length of time taken for his pulse to drop back to 60 beats per minute, to 50 and to 40 gives a clear indication of the extent to which he has improved in the interval.

(Many other physiological changes accompany increasing fitness. Race horse trainers check fitness by making packed cell volume (PCV) tests. These show the proportion of red blood cells to plasma in the blood. This measurement increases as the horse becomes more fit — it is the red blood cells which carry oxygen. There has, however, been some controversy as to whether or not the PCV of a long distance horse does increase with his fitness. Some experiments appear to show that, on the contrary, in Arabs trained for long distances it decreases. Other associated changes include an increase in the total blood volume and the utilization of additional blood vessels.)

The training programme

At every stage of his training the horse must be fed in proportion to the work done. Feeding is considered in Chapter 4.

Exercising periods at the start of training must be short and the work slow. All increases in both length and intensity of exercise must be gradual. Two short spells in a day are better than one long one.

A horse which has been turned out for some three weeks starts work at a walk, but this walk must be brisk. Some riders consider that he should not be ridden at a trot until he is walking ten miles a day. By this time he will probably be due for a day's rest. Throughout his training he will be worked for several days at a time and then rested for a day or two. How many days he should work between one rest and the next, and how long each rest should last, can only be decided as his training progresses. It is a help to draw up a time schedule before starting to train a horse, but the times allowed can never be more than provisional. Rest must never be total, the horse being confined in a box with nothing to do and a lot to eat. He must be turned out for short periods, exercised in hand or ridden more slowly than usual. His rest must in fact be relative to the work he would otherwise be doing. His feeding must be reduced proportionally. Each time a horse is rested his fitness decreases slightly; when he resumes work, it first regains its former level and then improves further.

When hills are accessible, full use should be made of them. Walking and trotting up hill greatly strengthens a horse's legs and an uphill trot can increase the demand on heart and lungs as effectively as a gallop on the flat. This form of exercise, therefore, is particularly useful early in his training, when a gallop would place too much strain on his legs.

A horse that has already done two or three week's work (we are talking of course about a horse that has started training after only a short rest) can be exercised to improve his fitness on any one day either moderately hard for one long continuous spell (see Glossary) or very hard for a series of short spells

49

interspersed with intervals of rest or of work at a greatly reduced level of intensity.

For the latter system the rider must be able to check pulse
rate. It is not difficult to learn to use a stethoscope (it has been
said that many riders in the United States would be more lost
without their stethoscopes than without their jeans), but the
rate can also be checked by placing a hand over the horse's
heart behind his elbow, or by feeling the pulse under his jaw
or inside the front leg below the knee.

The procedure in this system of training is as follows: the
horse is galloped on the flat or ridden smartly uphill at a speed
which it is difficult for him to maintain. As soon as he begins
to flag, the rider pulls up, dismounts and checks his pulse. This
must record more than 80 beats per minute. If it records less,
then the work will have been insufficient to improve his fitness.
When the pulse has dropped back to 60 or less the rider re-
mounts and the exercise is repeated.

Experience soon enables the rider to correlate a particular
horse's feel and look with his pulse rate, so that after a while it
will no longer be necessary for him to dismount to check it.
But he should confirm his guess from time to time.

This method of training has the great advantage that it allows
a horse to work exceedingly hard without the likelihood of any
ill effects. This is because the frequent resting intervals avert the
danger of his muscles becoming seriously short of oxygen and
of extreme overheating leading to dehydration and its attendant
ills. These dangers will be discussed in Chapter 5. However, a
long distance horse cannot be trained entirely in this way. He
must sometimes carry a rider fast for long periods at a time,
since this is what he will have to do on the ride itself.

Swimming is excellent for increasing the fitness of all horses
which do not suffer from weakness in the stifle joints. Some
horses whose stifles are quite strong enough for long distance
rides might still be injured by swimming.

Horse walkers have been used with great success in the
United States, Britain and South Africa. They save time, in that
they allow one person to 'lunge' four horses (with some models

six) simultaneously and at both walk and trot. But they must always be used with discretion; the horses' headcollars must be attached at the right tension and the direction of circling frequently changed. They must not be allowed to take over a training programme; a horse on a walker improves in fitness, but he does not at the same time become accustomed to carrying his rider's weight for hours at a stretch, nor does he learn to negotiate ride country. And sitting or standing by the walker does nothing to improve the fitness of the rider.

From time to time towards the end of his training the horse must be taken out for rides, which in both length and severity approximate increasingly closely to the event which is his ultimate aim — approximate, but never equal. The final trial for a 100 mile (160 km) ride run over a very difficult course could well be of the same distance over a very easy one, while for an easy 100 mile competition it could be 75 miles (120 km) of the same standard or slightly more severe. These distances should be ridden two weeks before the actual event.

Following each long training ride the horse is worked less strenuously for a while. During the final two weeks before a 100 mile competition light work should be the rule, broken only by one fast 40 mile (64 km) ride as a final exercise for his heart and lungs.

Much skill and experience are needed if a horse is to be at his best for a particular event. No horse remains at his best for long. If he is fit enough some time before the ride, he will probably have become insufficiently fit by the time the ride is run. It is believed that the impossibility of maintaining maximum fitness for any length of time is, at least partly, due to the behaviour of a horse's red blood cells. These have a limited life. As they age, they decrease in efficiency. If at some time in a horse's training the number of his red blood cells has suddenly increased, then a large number will age simultaneously. When this happens his fitness will decline and he will be incapable of reaching his peak again until these cells have died and others have replaced them.

Teaching the horse how to behave in the conditions which surround a Long Distance Ride

A long distance horse must be a good and experienced traveller. He needs to start a ride rested, so he must not arrive at base worn out. If he has always been transported by a considerate driver and never needed to brace himself quickly against fast cornering and the jolts of sudden stops and starts, he will be sufficiently confident, in box or trailer, to travel without fussing; he will not break into a sweat nor hold himself tense throughout the journey.

The horse must become accustomed to eating, drinking and resting in the kind of place where he will stop at halts and spend the night during the course of the event. In Britain, this may only mean spending the night in an unfamiliar loose box; in the United States, in Australia and in South Africa a horse may well have to remain tied to a trailer, to a picket line or in a roped-off corral. He must get used to drinking water from a variety of sources; water from home can no doubt be transported for him to drink over night and at halts, but he must also be prepared to drink freely from every source along the route.

He must settle well both in the company of other horses and alone. He must be easy for the veterinarians to handle. On all rides his temperature, pulse and respiration rates will be taken and his legs and back handled, when he must stand quietly. Failure to do so will lose marks on a competitive trail ride; on all rides it will use up energy, annoy his rider and the vets.

Training the rider
The rider must be as fit to ride his horse as the horse to carry him. An unfit rider greatly increases the difficulties of his mount. He tires quickly and so becomes not so much a rider as a burden, unable to adjust his weight to the vagaries of the route or afford his horse physical or moral support. Most riders become partially fit in the process of training their horses, but other physical work is necessary. On many endurance rides it may be necessary to dismount and walk or run.

4 Feeding, watering, equipping and general care

Feeding

An adult horse which is neither working nor breeding is fed principally on grass or hay. These have a low feeding value in relation to their bulk and cannot provide sufficient nutrients for a horse in training, whose ration of grass or hay must be progressively decreased and replaced by concentrates.

The specific ingredients of both rations vary from one country to another. They are dictated partly by what feeds are available and partly by tradition. In Britain the hay ration is rarely, if ever, lucerne (alfalfa) and the corn is traditionally oats and bran. For the British horseman 'corn' means either oats or the concentrate ration as a whole; in other countries it normally means the grain which in Britain is called 'maize'.

By the time a 15 hand (152 cm) horse is fit to go 100 miles (160 km) in a day his hay will have been cut to between 8 and 12 lb (3·6-5·4 kg) and his corn increased to about 16 or 17 lb (7·2-7·7 kg) — depending partly on his breed and conformation. It is always better to feed little and often. A large corn ration should be divided into three, or, preferably, four separate feeds. These must be given at regular intervals and never immediately before or after work.

Every change in quantity and kind of food must be gradual. Different samples of oats and of hay usually vary considerably. Even the change from one delivery of proprietary cake to another should be made by mixing the last bag of the old with the first of the new. All food offered must be of the highest quality — free from mould and dust, which cannot fail to damage a horse's wind.

Although feeding must be both regular and consistent, it must also be varied. A horse which is fed heavily easily loses

This horse is wearing an Australian military saddle which both distributes the rider's weight along its full length and allows air to pass freely through the channel above the spine. The mohair breastplate can be seen hanging behind the horse's elbow. The saddle is very comfortable for both horse and rider.

his appetite. Both this, and his general health, is improved by a weekly feed of carrots and by boiled linseed, honey or molasses stirred into his corn. In Britain a bran mash is given whenever the dung shows signs of becoming hard, and when a horse arrives home tired and wet. Even at the peak of his fitness he should be allowed to graze briefly, to nibble at such vegetation as he fancies and the district and season afford. These will vary from country to country. In Britain they include the tips of brambles and rose-briars along the hedgerows. But care must be taken that he does not eat any of the poisonous plants, such as bracken and woody nightshade, which horses do not invariably dislike. Poisonous plants in the United States include arrow grass, bracken fern, poison hemlock and loco weed.

Long distance horses require a great deal of salt. Licks by themselves are insufficient so some salt must be added to food, but never to water.

Feeding has remained an art. The person who feeds well watches his charge carefully and can often tell when he is on the point of going off his food or when, unless his ration is increased, he will begin to lose condition, without waiting until these things actually happen.

Watering

Some riders and even some ride organizers believe that during work a horse should be allowed to drink only briefly, if at all, and that after work, if he has been ridden for a considerable distance, some hours should pass before he is again allowed to drink his fill. These views have in the past been responsible for the death of more than one animal. If a horse wants to drink, then this is because he needs to drink; if he wants to drink a great deal, this is because he is seriously short of fluid. It is true that an exceptionally thirsty horse must not be allowed to drink all he wants without stopping, but every attempt should be made to limit the number of occasions when he reaches this state.

Water must always be available in paddock and box. There will then be no reason for a horse to drink excessively immediately before a feed or before work, nor will he start work thirsty. Training rides should be arranged over routes where water is available at frequent intervals. On many competitions, because of the speed, the weather and the difficulties of the route, it will in fact be impossible to keep a horse so well watered that he arrives at each drinking place in a fit state to drink all he needs without a pause. In these circumstances it is essential that he should remain by the water, drinking at intervals, until his thirst is fully quenched. If he is taken away before he has drunk enough, he will be even more thirsty by the next time water is available. Not all riders are agreed exactly how much water can be allowed at each drink, nor how long the pause between one drink and the next should be. Dr Mackay Smith, a veterinarian, who is himself a very experienced long distance rider, has advised drinks of 15 to 20 swallows (which is between $\frac{1}{4}$ and $\frac{1}{2}$ a gallon (1-2 l)) and suggests pauses of one minute. He emphasizes the necessity of then riding the horse at a walk for a few hundred yards (metres), that is, until the water in his stomach has had time to warm up.

Reliable authorities do not yet agree on the danger of giving hot horses cold water. Some say there is no danger, but most riders can quote cases of ensuing colic, so the chill should be taken off whenever possible. Cold water is much less dangerous to a hot horse if he moves on immediately than if he has subsequently to stand about. Water from a cold stream or lake is better than no water at all.

Grooming

This should be thorough. The more vigorous form of grooming, called strapping, tones up a horse's muscles. All grooming supples and cleans the skin; by doing so it allows the process of sweating to cool the horse more effectively (see Chapter 5).

Meticulous care should be taken wherever the skin comes in contact with the saddlery — the areas beneath the saddle, girth and breastplate, if one is worn. Since long distance horses are saddled for longer periods at a time than other horses, they are more susceptible to girth and saddle galls; clean and supple skin does much to forestall these. The saddle area itself should be hardened with methylated spirits or with one of the proprietary preparations specially manufactured for this purpose.

After work the horse should always be made to feel comfortable. His feet should be picked out, his nostrils and the skin round his eyes and under his dock should be sponged. If the work has been strenuous, his legs should be bandaged.

General care

That a horse should never come in hot from exercise has long been accepted as a rule of good horsemanship. Walking the final mile or so brings him home safely cool and dry. However on long distance rides he will frequently arrive hot at a halt and at the finish. He will then require cooling (see Chapter 7). To this he must become accustomed during training. But he must never be brought home hot and left to dry off by himself.

If he is stabled, his box must always be clean and airy. But he is better kept in a bare paddock with a shelter, or preferably a box, where he can take refuge at will from the weather and the flies. In cold weather he will need less food if he is kept rugged.

56

Tequila, unregistered Thoroughbred gelding, winner of the 1978 Quilty.
(Australia)

Helpers washing down a horse on the April Fool's Day ride while the rider drinks a cup of tea. (Australia)

South African National Endurance Ride: halt.

Shoeing

A horse's feet must be regularly trimmed. Failure to do this results both in the frog losing contact with the ground, thus failing in its purpose of absorbing concussion, and in the angle at which the foot rests on the ground being changed, so that the stress is incorrectly sustained down the entire length of his leg.

A pad between hoof and shoe is of great value on all rides where they are permitted and the ground is hard or stony. Modern pads which take the precise shape of the underside of the foot not only protect the sole and frog from cuts and bruises but themselves absorb a considerable amount of concussion. At the same time they allow the frog also to fulfil this function in the normal way, since it remains in effective, though not direct, contact with the ground. Pads should be removed after a ride and not used during training since they allow the underside of the hoof to become soft.

Some riders shoe the front feet with the toes stubbed back. The foot can then roll over more quickly. But since this method of shoeing also shortens the stride, its value is controversial.

Saddlery

Everything that a horse wears must be light, simple, clean, supple and well fitting. It is particularly important to avoid unnecessary weight on his head. Although during schooling and early long distance training it may be necessary to use a running martingale and special bits, some time before he is ready to take part in a long distance ride he should have learnt to go well with the simplest of bitting or even without a bit at all. Bitless bridles, besides being light, have the advantage of making it easy for him to drink without sucking in air. There is no time to remove a bridle at every pool and stream. When a bit is worn, it should be buckled on so that it can be taken out of the horse's mouth without removing the whole bridle.

Saddles must fit perfectly. Pressure must be evenly distributed over the panel; there must be none on withers or spine. Air should be able to pass freely through the channel above the spine. Since the shape of a horse's back will change a great deal

A bridle specially made from very light rope to reduce weight on the horse's head and so keep the point of balance well back.

during training, a constant watch must be kept to make sure that the saddle still fits. Breast plates may be necessary on some horses in hilly country. These are best made of mohair or leather covered with sheepskin. Girths and saddle pads are made from widely varying materials. Individual riders have strong preferences among these; but whatever is chosen, saddle pads must not draw the horse's back and both must be easy to clean. If weight must be carried on a ride, the horse should become accustomed to carrying it in weight cloths during training.

Rider's clothing

This must be comfortable and above all loose, so that air can circulate and sweat evaporate freely. In hot weather felt hats can be soaked in water and so help to keep the rider cool. Footwear should be easy to walk or run in. Many riders now wear gym or running shoes. But these have two disadvantages: being heel-less they offer no protection against a wet foot slipping through a stirrup, and being soft soled they allow the foot to feel the iron; some riders find this tiring. Whenever ride rules make some particular form of dress obligatory, the rider should become used to the prescribed clothes — hard hat, heeled shoes, etc. — during training.

60

5 Dangers that face the horse

In steeplechasing, a horse, however suitable, well trained or carefully ridden, risks being brought down and injured by another who crosses or falls in front of him. Long distance riding has no such unavoidable hazards but the very word 'endurance' warns riders and ride organizers that both knowledge and care are needed if the horses taking part are to suffer no ill effects.

The specific danger for the long distance horse is exhaustion. This is not to be confused with the extreme weariness and muscular fatigue which can easily result simply from a horse carrying his rider at no great speed, over going of no great difficulty, for a very long time. By the end of this time his stride may have become short and jerky and he may be so tired that he hardly knows where to put his feet. True exhaustion arises only when a horse exerts himself so strenuously that his heart and lungs are unable to keep up with his muscular demands. No rider can be unaware that his horse is overtired, an inexperienced one may miss the first signs of impending exhaustion.

When a horse exerts himself beyond the limits of his proper capacity, his physiology progressively fails him in two ways. His muscles no longer receive sufficient oxygen to release the required energy with impunity, and he has increasing difficulty in keeping himself sufficiently cool. These two failures between them give rise to a number of abnormal symptoms and conditions: sustained high pulse and respiration rates; 'tieing up'; thick, patchy sweating, and eventually inability to sweat; muscle tremors and 'thumps'; and colic. In the end they may lead to irreparable muscle and kidney damage, heat stroke, pulmonary oedema and heart failure.

On a long distance ride a high pulse rate indicates that a horse is short of oxygen, and a high respiration rate that he is too hot.

Failure to keep the muscles adequately supplied with oxygen
This leads to a certain disruption of the processes whereby muscular fuel releases energy, resulting in an abnormally high level of lactic acid in the muscles concerned and in the blood. A heavy accumulation of lactic acid in certain groups of muscles in a horse's hindquarters causes them to go into spasm. The horse is then said to be 'tied-up', or 'set fast'. The muscles affected are painful to the touch; the horse sweats profusely, is in great pain and barely able to move his hind legs. It should, however, be noted that when a horse 'ties up', the oxygen shortage in the affected muscles is by no means always because at that very moment they are working so hard that they require inordinately large amounts of oxygen to release the energy needed. The horse may in fact be standing still, but the blood vessels supplying the muscles have contracted so much that it is impossible for his heart to pump through them even a normal volume of oxygen-carrying blood. This may be a consequence of prolonged downhill travel or of chilling. Such chilling can result when the quarters are exposed to a cold wind after work or when they are washed down with cold water.

Tying up is always a serious condition and must be treated as such. When the accumulation of lactic acid reaches a certain level, it permanently destroys parts of the muscle, and when the myoglobin released in this destruction reaches the kidneys it causes damage from which the horse may die. Nearly all ride organizations warn competitors that a tied-up horse must never be moved. If he cannot be reached by motor transport, he must remain where he is. Movement greatly aggravates the condition and extends the area of muscle affected. These points are emphasized here because some writers state that if a tied-up horse is walked for half an hour his symptoms will usually disappear; but these writers are not in fact referring to 'tying-up' or 'set fast' as these terms are understood by the long distance rider, only to a form of cramp. (A case of tying-up is sometimes described as one of azoturia, a word more normally reserved for a condition which, though symptoms and results are the same, arises in different circumstances: i.e. when a fit horse resumes work after being confined without exercise on full corn feeds. Since the 'work' may be no more than walking across a yard, it may seem puzzling that he should suffer in the same way as an overexerted animal. The explanation appears to be that the affected muscles have stored large quantities of glycogen during the corn fed rest and that the subsequent demand for energy is then met by a breakdown of this glycogen *only*. Since energy release from glycogen is always anaerobic, large quantities of lactic acid quickly build up in the muscle with the same results as if no oxygen had been available.)

Muscles other than those of the hindquarters may also be affected by shortage of oxygen and consequent build up of lactic acid. Heart muscle itself may be so destroyed. The general term for such muscle damage is rhabdomyolysis.

Difficulty in keeping sufficiently cool

A horse suffers adversely both when he fails to cool himself sufficiently and when his cooling system works overtime.

On a cool day a horse which is only moderately too hot loses enough heat as air passes over the surface of his skin and fills his lungs. Whenever these methods of cooling prove inadequate, he sweats, thereby covering part of the surface of his skin with moisture, which then evaporates off from it. Heat is used up when moisture evaporates into the atmosphere, so that the surface from which it has evaporated is always left cooler.

By the time a horse has sweated 5 gallons (22 l) of moisture which he has not replaced by drinking, he is dehydrated. Since the fluid lost comes from his blood, this will now be thicker and so more difficult for the heart to circulate. From this point on his muscles will become increasingly short of oxygen and it will also be increasingly difficult for him to lose heat. This last is partly because the heat now takes longer to reach his skin and lungs, and partly because less fluid is left for him to sweat with and what sweat he can still produce is thick and evaporates less readily. Eventually he will be unable to sweat at all.

Dehydration in a hot horse is avoided in two ways. First, he may be allowed to drink enough water to replace all that he has lost; how much at any one time we have discussed in Chapter 4. Secondly, he can be bathed in water and so provided with what might be regarded as artificial sweat, though cold water must always be kept well away from the area over his heart, from his loins, his flanks and the muscles of his hindquarters. In fact in warm weather both methods must usually be resorted to. The second has the advantage of limiting electrolyte loss.

Electrolytes are constituents of the blood plasma — the liquid part of the blood from which the sweat is derived. They include sodium, magnesium, calcium and potassium. That they should be present in the horse's blood in the correct proportions is essential to the proper functioning of his metabolism. When blood plasma is lost in sweat, so too are the electrolytes which it contained. Drinking will rehydrate the horse, but unless electrolytes are added to the water it will do nothing to rectify their loss: the blood will regain its normal fluidity, but its electrolyte content will have been diluted. Shortage of electrolytes is responsible for some of the symptoms of exhaustion. Quivering of the muscles results from a lack of calcium and 'thumps' (synchronous diaphragmatic flutter), when a horse's heart appears to be beating in his flanks, is usually attributed to an insufficiency of calcium or potassium.

A horse which is finding difficulty in keeping cool by sweating tries to lose additional heat via his lungs. For this purpose he breathes in a series of short, shallow pants, not the long, deep breaths he uses when he needs large quantities of oxygen. It is this which causes the rise in his respiration rate.

Heat exhaustion follows when a horse fails for a considerable time to keep his temperature down reasonably close to normal.

Keeping cool is obviously more difficult in hot weather than in cold, since the air which circulates over the horse's skin and is drawn into his lungs is nearer to the temperature of the blood which has to be cooled. Thus he resorts sooner to sweating. But sweating is more effective in dry weather than in humid. Sweat can only evaporate slowly into an atmosphere already laden with moisture; which is perhaps the principal reason why horses have thriven in the desert and died in the jungle.

6 How are the dangers avoided?

The history of long distance riding is one of increasing desire among those taking part to avoid harm to their horses, increasing knowledge of how this can be achieved and increasing application of this knowledge by ride organizers, veterinarians and the riders themselves. Today the success of a ride as a whole is no longer judged by the winner's speed (though this is important to the individual rider), nor by how many of the competing horses finish within the maximum time allowed; but on how few of these are any the worse for their efforts, and on how few of those which retired *en route* were not nearing exhaustion but merely tiring or suffering from some minor injury.

The early attempts

Death from exhaustion was once a common fate for a horse. When riding or driving was the only means of land travel faster than going on foot, a horse's life was counted but a moderate price to pay for arriving at a destination or delivering a message quickly in an emergency. The equine heroes of history covered remarkable distances, hardly pausing to draw breath — Roland from Ghent to Aix, Black Bess from London to York, Somerset from Durban to Grahamstown and many others: all died as the result of their exertions. Attitudes began to change, though not everywhere, after the coming of the railways enabled men to go faster by train than on horseback or in horse drawn vehicles Horses were of necessity still regarded as expendable during military campaigns, but, this apart, valid reasons for riding or driving a horse to death were gone. Thus, when in 1892 and 1901 races between Berlin and Vienna, and Brussels and Ostend, resulted in deaths of 25 and 30 horses respectively, there was an uproar in the British press. From then on the organizers of nearly all long distance rides and races, in the majority of countries where these were held, have been aware of the need to guard against the possibility of such tragedies.

Up to World War II perhaps the most common, and probably the most effective precaution taken was limiting the average speed at which a horse might travel. In the non-race type of ride speed was limited throughout. In the race type, normally then spread over several days, it was limited during the earlier stages. For a three day ride, for instance, it was believed that a limit on the first and second days would eliminate the unfit horses, with no harm done, while those still in good order on the eve of the final day would have proved themselves sufficiently fit to complete the course at whatever speed their riders chose. In addition, horses were sometimes examined before the start to see whether they were fit enough to compete at all, at the end of each daily stage to see whether they were fit enough to continue the following morning and at the finish to see whether they were fit enough to be awarded a prize. However, since at that time relatively little was known about exhaustion, the latter precautions were much less effective than they are today.

There were few long distance rides anywhere during the immediate pre-war years; nor was the sport revived as soon as the war was over. They were still uncommon in 1955, the year of the first Tevis, the starting point of the great popularity of long distance riding in the United States. By this time, however, the need for precautions and the lessons learnt earlier in the century had largely been forgotten; so that for a while the new rides were run almost without rules. Initially, since the riders taking part were mostly experienced horsemen, little damage was done, but as the sport became more popular so the number of competitors with only limited experience increased and with it the need to protect the horses. Rides began to include veterinary supervision, compulsory halts and strictly enforced rules.

Long distance riding was not effectively revived in Britain until 1965. The following year saw its first beginnings in Australia. In Britain the majority of organizers were profoundly

South African National Endurance Ride 1976: Sahibi Shaikh Hamed and
Sahibi Rifaa, the two Arab full brothers and joint winners, galloping over the
Free State plains.

Sahibi Shaikh Sulman, photographed three days after his 1977 win. (S.Africa)

The Golden Horseshoe Ride 1977: crossing the Barle at Tarr Steps. (Britain)

The Golden Horseshoe Ride. (Britain)

The Summer Solstice 100 mile (180 km) Endurance Ride 1975. At every source of water horses must be allowed to drink. (Britain)

aware that hazards existed against which precautions were necessary. But they were also wholly without experience and curiously ignorant of all the valuable information which had accumulated over the preceding ten years in the United States. The Australians, on the other hand, were both experienced and well informed. Some of those responsible for the organization of the first Quilty had themselves competed in the Tevis. They learnt all they could about long distance riding as it was organized in the United States and then adapted the best of American practice to suit their own needs. From this Australian long distance riding has benefited greatly.

The methods by which horses are protected today

Since 1965 communications between long distance riders and, perhaps even more important, between long distance veterinarians has increased throughout the English speaking part of the world. For this reason the main outlines of the systems whereby long distance horses in these areas are protected are now very much the same. But the details vary, not only from country to country, but from ride to ride. This is significant since quite a small variation in the criteria used to decide whether a horse should be withdrawn from a ride or allowed to continue can have a very great effect on the number of horses completing the ride in safety.

Veterinary procedure

The team examines the horses before the ride, on the course at both halts and spot check points, at the finish and, when awards are made for finishing condition, again some time later.

The inspections before, during and after the ride serve their purposes in different ways. The pre-ride inspection prevents from starting horses which are judged likely to be in difficulty before they even reach the first check point. These include those which are lame, or in view of the state of their legs, feet or shoeing likely to become lame; those which are unfit to carry a saddle because their backs are tender or because they have girth or saddle sores; those which are unfit to ride in a bit because they have sore mouths which preclude bitting and are untrained to go in a hackamore, those which are suffering from abnormal heart or respiratory conditions or from any other form of illness, and also those which the rules make ineligible.

So far as preventing exhaustion is concerned this preliminary examination is useful only in that it enables the veterinary team to record for future comparison each horse's resting pulse and respiration rate and the way he looks and behaves before he has started work, while the one at the end of the ride protects the horse only by acting as a deterrent to those who might otherwise have been tempted to push their animals too hard on the final section of the route. Such riders will be more careful if they know that winning an award depends on their horses being passed 'fit to proceed'. This examination also allows identification of horses in need of veterinary attention. It is at inspections made during the ride that horses in danger are detected and withdrawn; the standards applied at them are critical.

When ride organizers first enlisted the help of veterinarians, these were expected merely to find out when horses were either already exhausted or rapidly becoming so. Today most ride organizations ask much more of the veterinary teams — they are expected not simply to detect exhaustion, but to prevent it ever occurring. Thus the description of standards to be used by veterinarians officiating on behalf of the Australian Endurance Riders Association states: '*It should be remembered that we are attempting to establish which horses are fit to proceed and those which, if allowed to proceed would become exhausted. In other words the criteria are designed to predict those which will become exhausted before this happens.*' This point is again emphasized in a statement which reads: '*We are trying to ensure that a horse passed OK to go on is likely to arrive at the next check point in fit condition.*'

What the vets look for

The team can tell much simply from looking at the horses. We have already mentioned some of the adverse symptoms in the

A veterinarian takes the pulse rate of a horse just arrived at a halt. Note that this horse, in hard training, is very well muscled and does not give the impression of being thin. Malibou Mountain Ride (USA)

A veterinarian takes the pulse rate of a horse which has rested at a halt for half an hour. The horse is relaxed but bright. He shows every sign of having been thoroughly washed, cleaned and groomed. Note the towel still protecting his loins and croup. April Fool's Ride (Australia)

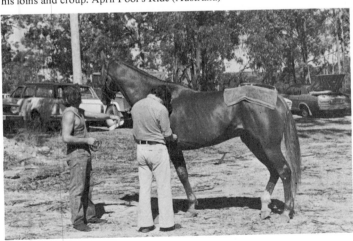

preceding chapter. In addition, all tiredness is accompanied by general listlessness and lack of desire to eat or graze. The early onset of tieing up is seen in the way a horse moves — though it may require an experienced eye to distinguish between the first signs of tieing up and those of incipient colic. A horse whose muscles are seriously short of oxygen may breathe so slowly that he takes less than one breath per stride; in one that is also overheated short breaths will be interspersed between long ones until oxygen needs are met, after which they will become almost continual. Dehydration, is indicated not only by thick, patchy sweat and failure to sweat, but also by the loss of the red colour from the mucous membrane round his eyes and gums, since thick blood limits its circulation through smaller blood vessels.

Thus careful visual examination already provides the veterinarians with much useful information. The use of further, non-visual criteria then serves to confirm what they already believe or suspect; to provide better evidence as to how seriously a horse is affected and to bring to notice any animal whose degree of distress is so mild that he shows no obvious symptoms. The temperature is taken to establish the degree to which the horse is overheated. If a finger is pressed against his gum and the depression so made takes a long time to fill out, this is a sign that his blood is too thick to flow back at the normal rate, also indicated when a fold of skin on his neck, pinched between finger and thumb, fails to flatten out quickly — if this takes more than 5 seconds, then he is moderately to severely dehydrated. (Long distance riders often make use of this test themselves as they go along.) On more sophisticated rides blood samples may be taken and analysed to give a fuller picture of both dehydration and electrolyte loss. (A packed cell volume test, showing the proportion of cells to plasma, gives the degree of dehydration with some accuracy, allowing that during exertion additional red blood cells are released into the blood stream by the spleen to allow it to carry more oxygen.)

The significance of pulse and respiration rates
The pulse and respiration rates are taken on arrival at each halt

and again after an interval which is usually half an hour but on some rides 20 minutes. This interval has no relation to the time a horse is required to remain at the halt to rest. It represents the maximum length of time which the veterinarians who advise the ride organizers think can safely be allowed for these rates to fall to an acceptable level. The overriding importance attributed to P/R readings is shown by the fact that every major ride publishes, as part of its ride results, P/R readings for every horse 'in' and 'out' at every halt and the finish. ('Out' in this case does not mean at the time the horse leaves the halt, but when he is either passed 'out', i.e. fit to continue, or eliminated.)

Listening to a horse's heart immediately he arrives at a halt may show that it is beating irregularly, but the rate at which it is then beating considered by itself gives little indication of how stressed he really is. Pulse rate immediately after stopping work depends, as we saw in Chapter 3, on the intensity of the work immediately beforehand. A horse in excellent order may arrive at a halt with a rate in the 80s, 90s or even higher. The 1977 Haggin and Tevis Cup (see Chapter 1) winners arrived at the first checkpoint with pulse rates of 96 and 112 respectively. At this stage no comparison between the different horses can be drawn. A very fit horse who has trotted fast into the halt may register a higher rate than one approaching exhaustion who has walked for the last two miles.

A horse's resting respiration rate is given by Dr Throgmorton as between 6 and 16 (normally aroused, 16-24). It is thus much lower than his resting pulse rate, 28-40 (normally aroused, 32-48). During hard work, as we have seen, both rates rise. If the respiration rate actually overtakes the pulse rate, the horse is said to have an 'inversion'. At one time all inversions tended to be regarded as indicating some degree of exhaustion and therefore as grounds for eliminating a horse. It is now agreed that inversion on arrival at a halt is not significant unless both rates are exceedingly high. In hot weather great exertion immediately prior to a halt may temporarily send the respiration rate racing up above the pulse as the horse breathes rapidly to cool himself down. This is, in fact, more likely to happen in a fit than an unfit animal, since, having less oxygen debt to pay, he resorts sooner to the fast breathing necessary for cooling, and in addition, since his pulse rate will have risen less high, his respiration rate will have less far to climb to exceed it. The Haggin Cup winner, referred to above, arrived at the halt called Devil's Thumb with 'in' readings of pulse 76 and respiration 80 — an inversion — but his 'out' readings showed his pulse fallen to 51 and his respiration rate well below it at 20.

By the time the second readings are taken both rates must have fallen back to an acceptable level. What levels are acceptable? It is agreed that for respiration no precise figure can be given for all horses on all occasions. How rapidly a horse is breathing, even after half an hour's rest, is affected by the weather and the degree of his relaxation. Thus it is often left for each individual veterinarian to decide the level acceptable for a particular horse, at a particular halt, on a particular day.

Pulse rate is less affected than respiration rate by extraneous circumstances and, since it is generally agreed that the level to which this recovers provides the best single indication of whether or not a horse is fit to continue, very great importance is attached to what level a ride organization decides to make acceptable. Despite this, not all ride veterinary standards specify a precise figure, some veterinarians still believing that the acceptable rate for this too should be allowed to fluctuate, though to a lesser degree, with weather conditions and the severity of the course immediately before the halt.

However, some years ago the Australian veterinarian, Mr R. J. Rawlinson, was able to write that the horse with a pulse rate of '70 per minute or higher after a rest of 30 minutes has commonly proved to be unfit to continue, both on American and on Australian rides'. Although most rides now eliminate horses which do not recover to 70, one important event still maintains 80 as the acceptable standard. In 1976 experiments made by Dr Reuben Rose showed a close correlation between the incidence of various forms of exhaustion and failure to recover to a pulse rate of 60 or below by the end of half an hour. As a result of his work the Australian Endurance Riders

Association lowered the acceptable rate for the Quilty to 60 at the first halt and 70 at subsequent ones; it has recently reduced the latter to 65. Records show the best and fittest horses recover to well below 60. The 1978 Quilty winner recovered to 40, 43 and 45 at the first three halts and 47 at the finish. Lowering the acceptable rate leads to extra training. No doubt if all rides lowered it to 60, some horses would be eliminated which would have finished unharmed; other horses' lives might be saved.

Some riders, and even some ride organizers, do not yet fully understand the object of recording pulse and respiration rates for a second time. They think these second readings are designed to show which horses have already rested long enough and which require more rest before being allowed to go on, without realizing that a horse whose rates are too high at the second reading has already been shown unfit to proceed, a fact which no subsequent recovery can change.

The part played by the rider

Veterinary supervision of long distance rides has greatly increased the riders' own knowledge and with it their ability themselves to protect their horses. The rider being always with his horse is in a much better position to judge his fitness than a veterinarian who sees him only at intervals. He too can use the criteria used by the vets. The information provided by taking his horse's P/R readings between the two official checks at a halt is particularly helpful. If these start to fall rapidly soon after arrival and are down to the required level by the end of ten minutes, then he can decide to push on; if they take nearly the whole half hour to recover, he knows he will have to go slowly in order to avoid elimination at the next halt.

Horses are obviously more often in danger of being over-ridden in races and endurance rides than in trials and tests, since in these the awards are made partly for finishing in good order or remaining in good order throughout the entire competition. On competitive trail rides P/Rs are often checked 10 minutes after arrival at a halt, which allows the judge to give more marks to those horses which recover most quickly.

7 The ride itself

Preparations

Before even making his entry the rider must find out enough about the ride to know whether it is suitable for his horse, and later, sufficient to plan how it should be ridden. Some of the information he needs is provided by the ride rules, ride description, time table and map, some can be found in reports and results of rides in previous years and some learnt from discussion with riders who then took part. But he is much more likely to ride the ride well if he inspects the course; local competitors and those who have competed previously are always at an advantage. Ideally, he will ride over at least some parts before the day, learning from experience what plan is likely to work best and accustoming both his horse and himself to the route and the going. If time is short he should choose the final sections and those he will ride in the dark. It is near the end that the horse, now tired, is helped most by knowing his way, and if he has been over the last stretch more than once, he will take heart when he reaches it, knowing the finish is near. In Britain practice is rarely possible, as most rides cross private land.

For all but the shorter rides the competitor must be supported by willing and knowledgeable helpers. At each halt these must be waiting with everything he and his horse will, or might possibly, need, including water already warmed. (On some rides in the United States it is not permitted to heat water except by standing it out in the sun.) It may also on occasion be necessary for them to take water to agreed points between the halts. In Australia helpers may not assist between halts, but if a horse finds a bucket of water by the wayside he may drink it.

The Golden Horseshoe Ride. (Britain)

The Golden Horseshoe Ride: watering at a small stream. (Britain)

Horses training on a walker. (Britain)

An inexperienced rider will be less likely to arrive at base without something he needs if he makes a list of requirements some time beforehand. He should carry with him a hoof pick, an 'easy boot' and, except in really cold weather, a sponge: the easy boot is to replace temporarily a shoe if one is cast at a place where it would be difficult for the farrier to reach him; the sponge to bathe both his horse and himself — it can conveniently be attached to the saddle with a string and lowered into water without the rider dismounting.

Careful adjustment of both food and exercise during the final week are important for both horse and rider. Both must arrive at the start rested but in no way let down and both must have sufficient reserves of muscular fuel to see them through the journey. The horse stores some fuel in his muscles and liver, but if he carries no fat at all there will be none to resort to when these are depleted. He must not be stuffed with food before a ride, but he must have been eating well. Unfortunately it is not possible to build up a reserve of electrolytes, as any surplus to his current needs will be lost in his urine. It is possible, however, to make sure by a blood test that he is not already suffering from any deficiency.

Adjustment of exercise and diet can ensure that a rider is storing the maximum fuel in his muscles immediately prior to the event. Dr Irvin E. Farin has suggested that he should 'engage in heavy and prolonged exercise on the fifth, fourth and third days before a ride, eating a mixed diet of fat and protein. On the second and first day he should do only light work, eating a diet rich in carbohydrates.' (*Endurance Digest* vol 3 no 3 July/August 1974.) These he suggests should be in the form of fruit, whole grain bread, nuts, honey, etc.

The competitor must arrive at the ride base in time for the veterinary inspection and the pre-ride briefing, at which he will learn, among other things, the starting order and news of conditions on the route. But if the journey is long, and the accommodation for the horses at the base adequate, he is well advised to arrive a considerable time beforehand. All travel is a bad prelude to a ride.

Rider and runner in the Levi Ride and Tie. (USA)

Planning how to ride the ride and putting the plan into effect

In suiting his plan to the horse the rider must take account of how long he needs to warm up and at what pace he moves most freely and easily. Some horses, when fit, do not reach their best until they have been 50 miles or even further; they do badly when ridden fast near the beginning. Some are happier and more efficient at a trot than a canter, others at a canter than a trot. A horse's best pace should be used wherever the going is suitable, though on some rides there is little choice; the English Marathon race and nearly all 50 mile (80 km) endurance rides in the United States demand long periods of galloping and cantering from those who are trying to win. A fast trot is the common pace for most horses on rides of 100 miles.

In suiting his plan to the route the rider must bear in mind that maintaining a steady output of energy is more important than maintaining a steady speed. He, therefore, allows least time for the downhill stretches and those over resilient going; most for the uphill stretches and those over holding going.

In suiting his plan to the temperature and weather he allows least time for the stretches he will cover at night, in the early morning and late evening and most for those he will cover in the heat of the day; least for those where he can expect a breeze to be blowing, most for the valleys where the air may be still and humid.

He will often have to weigh one set of conditions against another; for example, if he enters a horse which goes best ridden slowly at the beginning for an event which, like the Quilty, starts at midnight, and where it is therefore important to put many miles behind during the first few hours.

The rider must allow time for stopping at water and plan to arrive at each halt some 40 minutes before it is due to close, so that he will not need to hurry if, for some reason, he falls behind his schedule.

When the day of the ride arrives he should neither abandon his plan without good reason, nor keep doggedly to any part of it which proves to have been founded on false premises. He must not be stampeded into going faster than he intended because other horses are overtaking him and he thinks that their riders must know better than he does — they may not, or their horses may require to be ridden differently from his. On the other hand, some parts of the course or the going may prove either easier or more difficult than he expected. Even if he knows the course well, recent weather may have changed the surface, the day may be hotter or cooler, his horse may be more or less fit. All these are good grounds for abandoning his intentions. He must also be prepared to dismount and lead his horse in places where this formed no part of the plan: when, for instance, the going proves unexpectedly difficult and his horse is tiring or when he himself is becoming stiff.

Horses are greatly helped by a rider who has good hands and correctly adjusts his weight. The rider must decide carefully when he should guide his horse and when he should allow him to choose his own way. It is by no means always the case that verges are preferable to tarmac; the latter causes more concussion, but the former make tiring going when they are either soft or uneven.

The very successful Pinto, Peanuts, cooling off on a Ride and Tie. Note that the water does not reach his loins and croup. (USA)

At the halts

Arrived at the halt the horse will usually need to make good an oxygen shortage and to cool down. He will also need to eat, drink, probably replace lost electrolytes, rest, be freshened up and generally made fit to continue his journey. Some of these things he can do for himself, for others he needs human help.

Unsaddling

Removing saddle and bridle and replacing them with a halter and rug as soon as a horse arrives greatly helps him to relax. But many riders are wary about off-saddling immediately. The area under the saddle has been compressed by the weight of the rider and by the girthed up saddle for a considerable time. If this has resulted in some blood vessels becoming constricted these will now be empty of blood. Sudden and total release from pressure can then result in the blood flowing back so fast that these rupture, allowing serum to leak into the skin where it forms what are rather confusingly called heat bumps. These may make it impossible to replace the saddle and continue on the ride. Riders with past experience of heat bumps often keep their horses saddled throughout the halt, excepting for the veterinary inspection; they may even tighten the girths initially to replace some of the pressure removed when they dismounted. If saddles fit properly and girths are not fastened too tight and the horse, having been well trained, is adequately muscled, no area of the back will be under such pressure that the blood vessels are ever without blood; so that a properly saddled horse can be unsaddled at once.

Rugging

Whether the horse should be rugged, and to what extent, depends on the weather and the degree to which he is sweating. He must cool quickly but without chilling. A cool breeze blowing over the surface of his skin when he is no longer moving is dangerous. In these circumstances he should be rugged immediately. Although many riders in the United States use close woven and voluminous sheets which cover the horse from head to tail, cotton mesh rugs appear to be the most satisfactory. These allow the air to circulate, but not to blow, over the body, so that the horse cools without becoming chilled. On a really cold day a further covering on top of this may be necessary in the early stages. When the weather is too warm to warrant rugging the horse completely, it may still be advisable to cover his hindquarters as a precaution against tieing up. Some riders think it wise in certain weather conditions to wash their horses piecemeal — exposing only part of their skin to the cold air at any one time.

We have already discussed the value of putting water on a horse to cool him down *en route*. At a halt washing serves both to cool and to clean him. If he is very hot, cold water and in extreme cases even ice (when permitted) may be repeatedly applied to the veins on his head, to the jugular vein, to the inside of his legs and under his tail. These places are then left wet for the water to evaporate off. Cold water, as we have already seen, must be kept well away from the area over his heart, from his loins, his flanks and all the muscles which have been working most heavily. If these are washed, the water used must be warm, as must the water used to wash under his belly.

Ride and Tie competitors travelling fast: Flying C Glaovi, an Arab, and Jim Remillard (*left*); Peanuts, a Pinto, and Chuck Stalley (*right*). (USA)

All these parts should be rubbed dry and indeed any part which does not happen to need water for cooling. Great care must be taken to clean properly under the saddle and girth. His legs and the saddle area may then be rubbed with methylated spirits (or its equivalent), which restores circulation, quickly evaporates and leaves the surface cool and fresh. Nostrils and round the eyes and dock should be sponged, feet picked out, scratches treated with an appropriate aerosol spray.

Resting

Much can be done to encourage the horse to rest. He should be led to a patch of grass or sand where he can urinate freely. The place where he is washed and groomed should be carefully chosen. It should be quiet, near to or far from other horses as pleases him best, out of the sun on a hot day, out of the wind on a cool one and as free as possible from flies.

Whether he should be allowed to rest completely or walked at intervals depends on whether and how quickly he is likely to stiffen up. Riders are sometimes advised to walk their horses on arrival and at frequent intervals throughout the whole period of the halt. But while a horse is walking he is not resting. Some of the most experienced riders have found that many really fit horses do not stiffen up in so short a period.

The best kind of rug for a horse to wear while cooling down, but it must be made of cotton. On a cold day he may need another covering on top.

Watering and electrolyte replacement

If a horse has been properly watered *en route* he will not arrive at a halt excessively thirsty. He can certainly be allowed $\frac{1}{2}$ to $\frac{3}{4}$ of a gallon (2·2-3·4 l) of water every five minutes until he has drunk his fill. Most riders believe that the water offered at halts and the end of the ride should not be cold if the horse is hot; now that the horse is no longer moving cold water in his stomach will be slow to warm up. While there is almost complete agreement that lost electrolytes must be replaced, there is little about which, in what quantities and by what method. Riders are well advised to consult veterinarians who have experience of long distance riding in the districts where they intend to compete.

Feeding

Food recently eaten provides a ready source of energy. It is no longer generally believed that a horse cannot make use of what he eats in intervals between spells of strenuous work. Some riders like to give both a small feed of concentrates to provide carbohydrates and some hay to provide free fatty acids after the carbohydrates have been used up. A horse's stomach must not, of course, be overburdened. Many riders prefer to offer corn, hay and grass and allow their horses to choose.

Saddlery must be cleaned; girths, saddle pads and breast plates replaced when necessary.

87

These four horses competing in the 1969 Quilty have already covered approximately 75 miles (120 km). All are still obviously alert and full of going. No. 2 is an Arab mare, Psyche, ridden by Ron Males; no. 37 a Part-Arab gelding, Zeus, ridden by Miss S. Scantlebury; no. 9 a Part-Arab gelding, Spade, ridden by Col Adams, and no. 1 an Arab stallion, Shareym, ridden by Dr Frier. They finished 6th, 7th, 8th and 9th respectively. (Australia)

At the end of the day

The treatment which a horse needs at the end of the day is in principle the same as at a halt, excepting that he should now be walked more to prevent his becoming unduly stiff by the following day. Riders are still sometimes advised that their horse should not be allowed all the water he will take till three or four hours have passed; that he should be left saddled for a considerable time and that he should be walked continuously for an hour or more. These precautions do not apply when an animal has been well trained, well saddled and well ridden. But riders are rightly advised not to leave their horses for long periods unattended.

The horse needs to rest; he should be washed or groomed, bandaged and rugged with the minimum of fuss. Later the string rug should be removed and replaced with an ordinary one, if the weather is cold. If the ride is to continue on the following day, the horse will need his normal concentrate ration. It is perhaps safest to divide this into several small feeds. Much less can be fed if the ride is over.

To travel a horse straight home after a ride is to ask him to go on working when he most needs rest. How long he should remain at base depends on the accommodation available and the length of the journey home.

The next ride

The horse must be allowed plenty of time to recover before he is asked to compete again. As during training, he is let down slightly and then worked up to a new peak. Opinions differ both as to how long an interval should be allowed between one ride and the next and as to how many rides may be ridden in one season. One very experienced authority has expressed the view that the interval between two 100 mile (160 km) rides should not be less than three weeks to a month, while for a season four 100 mile rides or two 100s and six 50s (80 km) suffice.

Many long distance ride organizations now offer prizes for horses whose long distance mileage over the years adds up to a certain figure — usually 1000 (1600 km), and a championship prize for the one which travels farthest during one season. These give the best horses due recognition. But the championship prize sometimes tempts a rider to enter his horse for one more competition, though he knows in his heart that his horse has had enough.

The end of the season

When the last ride of the year is over, the horse must be let down gradually. He cannot simply be taken home and turned out to grass still keyed up to hard, fast work. His training now goes into reverse. His periods of exercise get shorter and his feeds smaller, until he begins to lose muscle and put on fat and falls back into a state of mind which will allow him to settle down happily in his paddock or field.

Appendices — results of four principal rides

Appendix 1 The Western States Trail Ride — The Tevis (USA)
Results 1955 to 1978

Winners of the Tevis Cup — awarded to the fastest horse

Year	Rider	Horse	Sex	Age	Riding time	Breed
1955, 1956	Wendell Robie	Bandos	S	15 and 16	—	Arab
1957, 1958	Wendell Robie	Molla	M	9 and 10	—	½ Arab
1959	Nick Mansfield	Buffalo Bill	G	11	—	TB cross
1960	Ernie Sanchez	Marko B	G	13	—	Mustang
1961	Drucilla Barner	Chagitai	G	10	13.02	¾ Arab
1962	Paige Harper	Chief	G	6	14.33	¾ Arab
1963	Pat Fitzgerald	Ken	G	7	13.30	Arab
1964	Neil Hutton	Salalah	M	10	14.10	Arab
1965	Ed Johnson	Bezatal	S	6	11.38	Arab
1966	Bud Dardi	Pancho	G	10	12.46	½ Arab
1967	Ed Johnson	Bezatal	S	8	11.42	Arab
1968	Bud Dardi	Pancho	G	12	11.18	½ Arab
1969	Marion Robie	Hailla	M	8	12.57	Arab
1970	Donna Fitzgerald	Witezarif	G	7	11.49	Arab
1971	Donna Fitzgerald	Witezarif	G	8	12.35	Arab
1972	Donna Fitzgerald	Witezarif	G	9	12.42	Arab
1973	Donna Fitzgerald	Witezarif	G	10	11.53	Arab
1974	Hal Hall	El Karbaj	G	8	13.55	Arab
1975	Donna Fitzgerald	Witezarif	G	12	12.04	Arab
1976	Donna Fitzgerald	Witezarif	G	13	11.59	Arab
1976	Sam Arnold	Rush Creek Champ	G	8	11.59	Arab
1977	Hal Hall	El Karbaj	G	11	14.15	Arab
1978	Kathie Perry	Prince Koslaif	G	12	12.17	Arab

Winners of the Haggin Cup — awarded to the fittest finishing horse among the fastest ten

Year	Rider	Horse	Sex	Age	Breed
1964	Paige Harper	Keno	G	6	Arab
1965	Wendell Robie	Siri	S	6	Arab
1966	Frank Moan	Barney	G	7	TB-Quarter
1967	Bud Dardi	Pancho	G	11	$\frac{1}{2}$ Arab
1968	Paige Harper	Raskela	S	7	Arab
1969	Walter Tibbitts	Ruff Spots Banner	G	10	Appaloosa
1970	Suzanne Morstad	Rajah	G	6	$\frac{1}{2}$ Arab
1971	Vicki Anderson	Sheba	M	9	$\frac{3}{4}$ Arab
1972	Hal Hall	El Karbaj	G	6	Arab
1973	Minette Rice-Edwards	Bright Hope	M	8	Anglo-Arab
1974	Eva Taylor	Hugo	G	9	Mule
1975	Wiggy Wisdom	Narabi	G	8	Arab
1976	Sam Arnold	Rush Creek Champ	G	8	Arab
1977	William Fox	Hazz	G	5	Arab
1978	Hal Hall	El Karbaj	G	12	Arab

Abbreviations
S — stallion
G — gelding
M — mare
TB — Thoroughbred

Metric conversion
1 lb — ·45 kg
1 st — 6·45 kg

Appendix 2 The Tom Quilty Endurance 100 mile (160 km) Ride — The Quilty (Australia) Results. 1966 to 1978

Year	Rider	Horse	Sex	Age	Weight carried	Riding time	Breed
1966	Gabriel Stecher	Shalawi	S	5	160 lb min	11.24	Arab
1967	Sam Timms	Zig Zag	G	6	,,	11.07	unregistered
1968	Les Bailey	Jackass	G	8	,,	12.02	Australian stock horse
1969	John Coyle	Jackass	G	9	,,	11.35	Australian stock horse
1970	Les Coyle	Cindy	M	9	,,	11.38	unregistered
1971	Ross Webb	Stoney	G	8	,,	10.49	unregistered Part-bred Arab
1972	Warren Webb	Stoney	G	9	168 lb	10.37	unregistered Part-bred Arab
1973	Col Adams	Tumbalong	G	7	161 lb	10.26	unregistered
1974	Arthur Paterson	Bing	G	9	192 lb	10.14	Standardbred
1975	Erica Williams	Noddy	G	9	168 lb	10.05	Part-bred Arab
1976	Robert Thompson	Joe	G	9	168½ lb	9.32	unregistered Part-bred Arab
1977	Sam Timms	Tally-Ho	G	8	176 lb	9.20	Australian stock horse
1978	June Petersen	Tequila	G	9	163 lb	*13.26	unregistered TB

* The 1978 Ride was run over a new course. The route covered 108 miles (176 km) and included many additional climbs and descents.